CLASSICAL
ARCHITECTURE

CLASSICAL
ARCHITECTURE
THE LIVING TRADITION

DEMETRI PORPHYRIOS

OPPOSITE: Andronikos of Kyrrhos, Horologion, known as Tower of the Winds, Athens, c middle 1st century BC
ABOVE: Mnesicles and Callimachus, The Erechtheum, Athens, c 421-405 BC

McGraw-Hill, Inc.
New York•St.Louis•San Francisco•Auckland•Bogatá•Caracas•Lisbon•London•Madrid•Mexico•Milan•Montreal
New Delhi•Paris•San Juan•São Paulo•Singapore•Sydney•Tokyo•Toronto

For Erato

FRONT COVER: Fragment of frieze depicting head of Gorgon,
Temple of Apollo at Didyma, c 2nd century AD
BACK COVER: Andronikos of Kyrrhos, Horologion, known as Tower of the Winds,
detail, Athens, c middle 1st century BC

We would like to thank the following copyright holders for permission to reproduce texts in the Appendix: Harvard University Press, Plato, *The Republic,* HM Hubbell, *Cicero in Twenty-eight Volumes,* Pliny, *Natural History,* and Vitruvius, *On Architecture*; Dover Publications, New York, SH Butcher, *Aristotle's Theory of Poetry and Fine Art with a Critical Text and Translation of 'The Poetics',* and Eugène-Emmanuel Viollet-le-Duc, *Lectures on Architecture*; Everyman's Library, *The Complete Works of Horace*; Oxford University Press, GWF Hegel, *Aesthetics: Lectures on Fine Art*; Johns Hopkins University Press, GE Lessing, *Laocoön*; Cambridge University Press, Gottfried Semper,*The Four Elements of Architecture*; *9H,* Heinrich Tessenow, *House-Building and Such Things*

All colour images photographed by the author

Library of Congress Cataloging-in-Publication Data

Porphyrios, Demetri,
   Classical Architecture / Demetri Porphyrios.
      p.   cm.
   Published in Great Britain in 1991 by
ACADEMY EDITIONS an imprint of the Academy Group Ltd, 42 Leinster Gardens, London W2 3AN
   Includes index.
   ISBN 0-07-050478-4
   1. Architecture, Classical.   I. Title
NA260.P671992
722'.8--dc20   92-15369
                                                                                                      CIP

ISBN 0-07-050478-4

Printed and bound in Singapore

C O N T E N T S

ABOVE: G Trissino, Villa Trissino, Cricoli, c 1532-38

P R E F A C E

Over the years I have found myself increasingly concerned with problems of building construction and architectural form. Problems of practice and also of theory which, as it happens, presented themselves both in discussions with my university students and with my colleagues at my practice and on site. It is this preoccupation with the relation between building and architecture that initially stimulated and continues to nourish my interest in the classical.

Critics and practitioners of this century have paid little attention to the relation between building and architecture. Nor have scholars shown much interest in this subject except when it has been essential to research of a more antiquarian kind. In the Post-Modern seventies and eighties, many critics and practitioners flirted with classical imagery but I suspect very few had any working knowledge – and many not even a faint acquaintance – of the classics. Post-Modernism has been sustained essentially by questions deriving from contemporary post-structuralist literary theory. Keeping up with the fashion of the period, post-modernists grafted onto architecture literary concerns about language and representation. As a result and in the course of their polemics they lost sight of 'firmness, commodity and delight' and squandered their talents on the complacency of decorated sheds.

Now, to anyone studying the relation between building and architecture, classical architecture offers many opportunities. Indeed, I can think of no other architecture so promising in its treatment of this subject. At the same time, I have undertaken to think about the classical because the need to focus on the dialogue between building technology and architectural representation is becoming all the more urgent. The recent inclusion of modernist and deconstructivist nostalgia in the stylistic ranks of Post-Modernism means we will continue to witness the progressive deterioration of our cities and

OPPOSITE: Andrea Palladio, Villa Badoer, Fratta Polesine (Rovigo), c 1557

countryside alike. It is necessary, therefore, that the classical project is talked about afresh in an uncompromisingly modern way by architects and critics of a quite non-doctrinal formation.

The chapters of this book are reworked and expanded versions of six lectures in which the critical aspects of the classical are considered. I have been concerned less with offering a doctrinal interpretation of the classical than with showing how it exists in our everyday life today. My interpretations of the classical may not always be those of classical scholars, though I have drawn freely on their work. In the first chapter I examine the theory of imitation, the position it occupies in classical thought, and the way by which it can be shown that imitation is at the core of both traditional and modernist art. The second chapter is devoted to the significance of tectonics in architecture. In the third chapter I examine the relations between building and architecture and the way in which we may say that 'classicism is not a style'. The romantic theory of style is contrasted with the classical theory of character and in the fourth chapter I move on into the discussion of the significance of ornament. The fifth chapter addresses the principles of the traditional city and makes the claim for revitalising practical reason and common sense. The traditional city demonstrates the dialogue between continuity-and-change in human life and this brings me, in chapter six, to the discussion of tradition and originality.

Much of what I will be speaking of in this book will seem obvious enough. Yet it may throw some light on a fact we all know so intimately that we do not bother to ask questions about it: namely that there can be no building, no architecture, and no cities without the continuity of tradition. There are interesting side issues: why some buildings seem to exhibit a more enduring sense than others and why, on the whole, do the ones that seem more enduring so often turn out to be fairly old, not to say ancient?

The question of what can be said of a tradition – technological, representational or otherwise – inherited from the past is one of the most troubling issues of contemporary architectural criticism and practice. The history of traditions must in part be a history of error and of transient fashions but it would be a sort of arrogance for anyone to suppose that he can stand outside from that history and at the same time judge securely. It is a matter of fact that some traditions die while others survive. The one thing certain is that history is not a linear process of progress nor the sum-total of the 'spirit' of so many different ages. Instead what is more necessary – and perhaps convincing as well – is a view of history which is neither simply positivist nor simply historicist; but one which accepts that there exist such continuities as the culture elects to be its own.

This re-appraisal of sense that history affords through the mediation of tradition reminds me of a statement by José Carreras: 'We are not worried if other people have sung the same songs before. We use our talent, personality and feelings to bring something new to the music. In *pop* it is different. If you have a hit with a song, it becomes your own, but opera singers know that every night somebody sings the same work in a different opera house'.

Something similar can be said of classical architecture and generally of all architecture that is enduring. Working within a building tradition we find out, in Michelet's words, 'the knowledge we have of what we never learned and the memories of things we never witnessed; we feel the reverberation of the emotions of people we never knew'.

The lectures out of which this book originated were meant to make suggestions to my students and initiate discussion, rather than settle any of the problems raised. When I came to prepare these lectures in the form of this book, I had originally intended to write long explanatory and bibliographical notes. My publisher, however, suggested that this would probably destroy the directness of the argument and that perhaps I should keep notes to a minimum. Having thought about it, I did away with notes altogether. However, I could have not denied my intellectual debt to many previous thinkers and I opted, therefore, for including an extensive appendix comprising selected excerpts from texts which have influenced my thinking in a major way. There are, I realise, many more books which could have been included in the appendix; to those I owe a silent debt. Indeed, the volume of scholarship on classical art, architecture and the history of ideas is so enormous that I had better say that I have only Greek, Latin, French, and English. German sources I know only from translations. I have quoted the original Greek only when the argument required it and I have given it also in transliterated form.

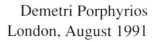

Firstly, I am indebted to the University of Virginia and Yale University at whose invitation the chapters of this book were initially delivered as lectures in 1987 and 1989. I am grateful to the respective Deans at the time, namely, Jaquelin Taylor Robertson and Thomas Beeby for granting me the privileges of Jefferson and Davenport professorships. I also have a long-standing debt to my publisher, Dr Andreas Papadakis, who has pioneered a context within which discussions about the classical could grow and become productive. I owe much to the controversy or agreement of a number of friends: Vincent Scully, Leon Krier, Alan Colquhoun, Charles Jencks, Jaquelin Robertson, Cesar Pelli, Harold Roth, and William Westfall. At universities in England, Spain, Scandinavia and America, I have found critical listeners who made me rethink my argument and to all those I am grateful. For their editorial competence, enthusiasm and tact I wish to thank Andrea Bettella, Annamarie Uhr, Helen Castle and James Steele. My special thanks go to Nigel Cox for his readiness in assisting with the proofs and the captions for the illustrations with perspicacity and sense.

ABOVE: Urn featuring carpentry tools of a tecton

Demetri Porphyrios
London, August 1991

CHAPTER I
IMITATION IN ARCHITECTURE

'The poet [. . .] like a painter or any other artist, must of necessity imitate one of three things: reality past or present; things as they are said or seem to be; or things as they ought to be.'
Aristotle, The Poetics

'There can be no social development which excludes all mythological relation to nature [. . .] and which accordingly claims from the artist an imagination free of mythology.'
Karl Marx, Introduction to the Critique of Political Economy

Whenever we visit or look at a building, we find our attention moving in two directions at once. One is pragmatic and is concerned with how the building functions. The other has to do with the nature of the building; in other words, we see the building as something that has been made. This is so since in human fabrication, in general, significance lies not in the utility or beauty that may accompany the artefact but in the recognition of ourselves as the makers of that artefact.

This recognition is essentially a contemplative experience and when viewed like this the building – though it may be useful – refuses to be used in any way. Architecture begins precisely here; it speaks of the usefulness which produced it in the first place, from which it detaches itself as art and to which it always alludes.

We may therefore ask: what is the nature and purpose of this detachment and what are the means by which it is achieved? In other words, in what sense can we say that architecture detaches itself from the contingencies of shelter and construction and, if so, why and how does it do that?

The conception of architecture (and art in general) as having a relationship to the world which is not direct but potential can be traced back to Greek antiquity. In his *Poetics* Aristotle discusses poetry and art as a form of truth liberated from experience: a response awakened in the observer by the transformation of experience and contingent reality into fictitious play. The central principle of Aristotelian aesthetics is that art is the imitation of nature. But what exactly are we to understand by the expression 'imitation of nature'?

The term 'imitation' (*mimesis,* the Greek μίμησις) has been so much used and misused in literary and popular discussions that its early Aristotelian meaning has been virtually lost. By the Hellenistic and Roman periods, the

OPPOSITE: Entry gate of House at Symi, c 1910

Poetics was not widely known and the major commentary which had taken its place was Horace's *Ars Poetica*. Working within a Hellenistic framework of thought that favoured the art of rhetoric, Horace distinguished between style and content and emphasised the former at the expense of the latter. The preservation of Aristotle's text was ultimately due to the literary cultures of Islam and Byzantium. The first printed edition of the *Poetics* appeared in Venice in 1508, and from then on a number of translations and commentaries were published during the Renaissance. Later, Neo-classicism turned the *Poetics* into codified, normative principles, at the same time elevating art into an idealised, metaphysical realm. With the advent of 19th-century romantic theories of genius, imagination and subjectivity, the *Poetics* lost its appeal, and by the time Brecht contrasted dramatic and epic theatre most of Aristotle's ideas were forgotten. In fact Brecht did what was expected of him by his time: he associated the *Poetics* with naturalistic, outmoded ideology and thereby dismissed it without seeking to understand Aristotle's principles of thought.

In a certain sense Brecht was right in suspecting the *Poetics* of outmoded clichés. Conventional opinion had often associated Aristotle's text with the generalisation 'art imitates nature' or with similar statements found in Renaissance treatises on poetry, art and architecture. In fact, interest in Aristotle grew much faster than accurate knowledge of his work and his ideas were often reduced to commonplaces. Similar commonplaces are still current today and I suspect that is why in everyday language the word imitation brings to mind copies and cloned replicas. Given our century's preoccupation with Modernist art, one can understand how such a naturalistic theory of art might appear suspect.

It is true that in his *Poetics* Aristotle writes that 'art imitates nature' (*e techne mimeitai ten phusin*/ἡ τέχνη μιμεῖται τήν φύσιν). But this could not possibly have the sense that art is a reproduction of natural objects, since for Aristotle nature is not the physical world that surrounds us, but rather the active force of the universe; in other words, nature refers to the principles which govern the world and make it possible. Indeed the inadequacy of the Latin translation 'imitatio' and the English derivative 'imitation' for the Aristotelian concept of *mimesis* (μίμησις) can be shown by a passage in the *Poetics* where it is mentioned that the artist imitates things as they ought to be (*oia einai thei*/οἶα εἶναι δεῖ). This passage shows clearly that imitation (*mimesis*) does not refer to a literal transcription of the world. It does not denote the servile duplication of the model; it is neither a copy nor a simulation of the physical world that surrounds us. Imitation here does *not* refer to a 'copy of a copy' as Plato would have it. Whereas for Plato imitation, in its recycling and endless repetitions, becomes a 'prison' and a threat to truth and order, Aristotle urges us to understand imitation as a cognitive practice that leads to knowledge about the world.

To imitate things as they *ought to be* means to represent something in a way that allows us to come closer to knowing it. Artistic imitation, in the Aristotelian sense, reveals the artist's (and our own as observers) preoccupations, concerns and criteria of evaluation. In that sense an imitation of the

ABOVE: K F Schinkel, The Invention of Painting, c 1841-47; OPPOSITE TOP & BOTTOM RIGHT: The origins of Architecture in Building: houses in Symi, c 1910; OPPOSITE BOTTOM LEFT: T Hansen, Athens Academy, 1859-87

world is always a transformation of the world, since what we select to represent through the work of art is necessarily what we have deemed to be relevant for representation. The central argument of the *Poetics* concerns imitation as a cognitive experience, as a mode of understanding and inhabiting the world. Imitation, in fact, being 'natural to man from childhood' shows us how to learn about the world and make it our own. At the same time there is a social dimension to be found in imitation: the recognition and knowledge it affords is never a mere arbitrary construct but speaks of our relations of reference to the world; and ultimately to the relations of power we are bound up with.

An etymological nuance throws further light on the Aristotelian concept of mimesis. We read in the *Poetics* that the artist imitates '*things* as they ought to be' (the italics are mine). Surely, Aristotle does not have in mind here 'things' as mere physical objects. Heidegger has pointed out that the old German word for *thing* becomes the name for an affair or matter of pertinence. In fact, the meaning of the Greek word for thing (*pragma*/πράγμα, from *pratein*/πράττειν, that which has been acted upon and therefore rendered pertinent) is still preserved in the English word as when we say, 'he knows how to handle things', or he knows how to deal with what matters.

The meaning of Aristotle is clear. What he wishes to show is that the artist imitates things as they ought to be (and therefore not necessarily as they are). What is more, he imitates no physical objects as such but rather 'things' in so far as they are the vehicles of an essential significance to him. It is in this sense that we can say that the Aristotelian concept of *mimesis* shows the way in which the world is true for us.

Consider for a moment Hume, who writes that 'the rules of architecture require that the top of a pillar should be more slender than its base . . . because such a figure conveys to us the idea of security . . .' (*A Treatise on Human Nature, II, I, iii*). The entasis of a column, however, does not follow the exact profile of the tree trunk. It comprises an image of nature's visual statics.

Consider also Le Corbusier: 'Let us reflect for a moment on the fact that there is nothing in nature that . . . approaches the pure perfection of the humblest machine: the tree trunk is not straight . . . If we say with certainty that nature is geometrical it is not that we have seen it; it is rather that we have interpreted it in accordance with our own framework' ('The Lesson of the Machine' in *L'Art Décoratif d'Aujourd'hui*). The Corbusian *pilotis* comprise an image of nature's geometricity by analogy with the machine.

In these examples, both Hume and Le Corbusier speak of the way in which the column imitates the tree. Neither of the two speak of actually reproducing a tree. Hume discovers in nature's workings an anthropomorphic image. Le Corbusier, on the other hand, discovers in nature a geometricity which is made pertinent by his admiration for the precision and exactitude of the machine. The classical imagination looks at the tree trunk and sees in it an image of stability which it commemorates in the form of the entasis of the column. Le Corbusier, aspiring to the attainment of mechani-

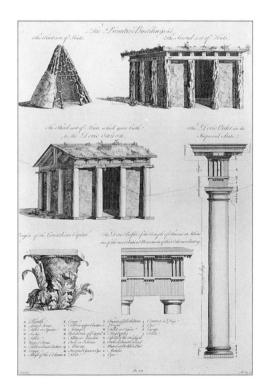

ABOVE: W Chambers, The Origins of Architecture in Construction, from his Treatise on Civil Architecture, *1759; OPPOSITE ABOVE: Le Corbusier, Villa Savoye, Poissy, 1929-31; OPPOSITE BOTTOM LEFT: T Jefferson, Pavilion III, University of Virginia, Charlottesville, c 1821; OPPOSITE BOTTOM RIGHT: G Asplund, Woodland Chapel, Enskede Cemetery, Stockholm, 1918-20*

cal geometricity, sees the tree trunk as a precise cylindrical form.

In both cases the artist imitates no physical objects as such but rather 'things' in so far as they have an essential significance for him. From one artist to another (or between different historical periods) the significance brought forward might vary and indeed it does: yet all art is imitation in the sense of representing in sensuous form the relevance that some-'thing' has for us. It is in this sense that we should understand the Aristotelian concept of imitation. *Mimesis* (imitation) discloses the way by which the world is true for us.

*   *   *

In what fashion does art speak to us? What are the means by which artistic imitation discloses the truth of the world for us? Does the work of art appeal to reason? Does it describe the world with concepts and discursive language? Aristotle reminds us here that a work of art is neither science nor philosophy but a likeness (*homoioma/ὁμοίωμα*) of some-'thing'.

Of the issues arising from the notion of artistic likeness a few demand special attention. In the first place, the notion of likeness points out that the work of art is always rendered in a sensuous medium (for example, paint, marble, sound, etc) and therefore speaks to us through the senses and not through the intellect. Art and architecture do not reach us by means of abstract reason but through our senses. Their medium is not discursive thought but sensuous form. The painter, Alberti reminds us, '. . . draws with lines and paints in colour . . .', and though there may be a body of theory and of practical rules which guide the artist, viewing a painting or visiting a building does not demand of us that we follow an intellectual argument or a logical disputation. The opening lines of Alberti's *Della Pittura* will remind us that none of this is new wisdom, when he says that: 'In everything we shall say I wish it to be borne in mind that I speak in these matters not as a mathematician but as a painter.'

I now turn to the second aspect that arises from the notion of artistic likeness. The question here concerns the nature of the medium in which the artefact is made as contrasted to that of its model. Indeed, when we say that a work of art is a likeness of the model we expect that the artistic medium is materially different from that in which its model is fashioned in the first place. A sculpture of a maiden does not use the maiden in flesh, nor does it attempt to render the folds of her dress in real cloth. The emphasis of the Aristotelian notion of likeness here is to extricate the idea of artistic imitation from the Platonic impasse of 'reduplication'. The image (*homoioma*) of the world that the work of art fabricates can never be a literal copy for it is always fashioned in a medium that is materially different from that of its model. Instead, the likeness that derives from the organic repetition of nature or from the mechanical repetition of industrial production has nothing to do with the likeness of artistic imitation. That is so, 'simply because', writes Quatremère de Quincy, 'that which constitutes the primary condition of imitation is wanting: namely the image'.

Similarly in architecture, a column does not render the bark of the tree with the moss growing on it. This is an obvious point and yet, so often, we

ABOVE TOP: Hellenistic statues from Pergamum Museum, Berlin; ABOVE BOTTOM: P Rubens, Saturn Devouring his Children, Prado Museum, Madrid; OPPOSITE: Lion devouring a horse, from a pagan sarcophagus, Vatican Museum, Rome

tend to forget the necessary *distance* that artistic likeness demands. The identical repetition of the model can only occur in mechanical cloning and for that very reason it does not afford us pleasure. On the contrary, artistic pleasure proceeds only from comparing the image with the model so that we may reflect upon that which has been deemed essential for representation. Artistic likeness, therefore, does not attempt to embody in the image the empirical reality of the things it sets out to represent. Instead, 'the aim of imitation in the arts is to represent reality by means of an image', writes Quatremère de Quincy. And yet, he continues, 'the greatest and commonest of errors consists of confounding resemblance by means of an image with similarity by means of identity'. I am reminded here of a postcard I once saw in Spain, a colour photograph depicting two flamenco dancers. Its author must have found the photographic impression wanting and, eager to 'enrich it', he added real lace for the lady's skirt and silk for her blouse. Somewhere, I am sure, there must be an 'improvement' of this postcard where the castanets can be heard aloud and the aroma of the Sevillian dusk touches our nostrils.

We know of course that this is kitsch. For kitsch promises us a world by 'inducing a hedonistic relaxation as a compensatory strategy' (Adorno). The aim of art, however, is not to deceive but to represent. In that sense, the difference between kitsch and art is that kitsch simulates as a compensation for that which is not; art imitates in order to distance itself from that which is and thereby throw new light onto it. This distancing is not a sign of ineptitude on the part of the artist but, rather, a crucial characteristic of artistic production as such. By distancing the artefact from its model, the artist invites us to see what we have never seen before, pointing out a relevance that might otherwise have gone unnoticed. This distance which art establishes between the world and the images it fabricates is at the very core of the experience of recognising the new and the relevant that art offers us. In this sense, the Formalist theory of *ostranenie* with its emphasis on the cognitive function of defamiliarisation is by no means incompatible with the classical aesthetics of imitation. The pleasure of recognition that the artistic image affords us is the very pleasure that accrues when art opens up for us a new access to the world; an access free from simulation and all stifling commonplaces.

What the work shows is elicited from contingent reality and is brought forward for our contemplation. There is enough resemblance with the model for us to understand what the work refers to; the rest is all 'truth'. To return to our earlier examples: the entasis of a classical column makes us see, in the diminishing girth of a tree trunk, nature's law of stability. On the other hand, the cylindrical form of the Corbusian column makes us see a projected geometricity of nature and thereby the machine as *bella natura*. Art and architecture construct a new world by both preserving and cancelling out the contingent world of our everyday life. The artist imitates the world by distancing himself from it and thereby discloses the way in which the world is true for him. If, or when, we find such truth relevant to ourselves, we rejoice and call the work beautiful.

ABOVE TOP: Postcard of flamenco dancers; ABOVE BOTTOM: Post-Modern still life; OPPOSITE: Palladio, Tempietto Barbaro, Maser (Treviso), c 1580.

The third aspect of the notion of artistic likeness concerns the common understanding of likeness as *trompe l'oeil* illusionism. In naturalistic theories of art it is assumed that the excellence of a painting corresponds to the faithfulness with which a painted representation matches reality. Pliny, for example, records the story of the contest between Parrhasius and Zeuxis. The latter painted a bunch of grapes and birds flocked to peck them. Parrhasius then painted a curtain so realistically that he deceived Zeuxis, who asked for it to be drawn so that he might see the picture behind it. Similarly, Vasari tells the story of the young Giotto who painted a fly onto a picture by his master Cimabue so convincingly that Cimabue was deceived and made a gesture to drive the fly away.

These and similar examples have confused artists and critics alike. For if, as we have seen, imitation underlines the distance between the work of art and its model, how are we to account for the practice of naturalism? The contest between Parrhasius and Zeuxis may at first mislead us since it might wrongly be taken to promote the idea of art as deception. But such anecdotes from antiquity or the Renaissance were meant to serve as examples of virtuosity in draughtsmanship and exactitude of execution (*akribeia*). Had naturalism aimed at deception it would have not resorted to the conventions of painting but would have taken up sensuous verisimilitude and would have transgressed the boundaries of the different arts. Instead, classical antiquity insisted on the demarcation of the arts based on the different medium that each art used. Imitation, therefore, in the classical Aristotelian sense, has nothing to do with the literal verisimilitude of simulation nor does it aim at deception. Nor for a moment does artistic imitation leave us in doubt about the fact that it intends to portray what is essential and significant; not merely what appears as duplicity. Imitation (the likeness of) does not involve the false belief that we are in the actual presence of what the image represents. Instead, we approach the work of art as an image of the world which the artist has judged to be especially worth bringing to our attention. In fact, this image of the world which the work of art presents to us is always a typical representative example (*paradeigma*/παράδειγμα) which is invested with an equally representative value.

Still more important is a further qualification that Aristotle places on the idea of imitation. 'Since the poet, like the painter or any other image-maker, is a mimetic artist (*mimetes*/μιμητὴς),' Aristotle writes in his *Poetics*, 'it follows that he must produce a mimesis of one of three things: reality past or present; things as they are said or seem to be; or things as they ought to be (*oia einai thei*/οἷα εἶναι δέι)'. Aristotle frees artistic imitation from the burden of literal transcription of material reality to which Plato had tended to restrict it. Art not only need not imitate things as they are, but it may be concerned with things as they ought to be. The example of the maidens of Croton is pertinent here. When the citizens of Croton commissioned Zeuxis to paint a cult image of Venus he chose as his model not one but the five most beautiful maidens of the city so that he might represent in his painting the most praiseworthy features in each of them and make therefore an image of Venus as it ought to be.

ABOVE: Temple of Vesta, Forum Boatium, Rome, c 50 BC; OPPOSITE TOP LEFT: Stoa of Attalos, door detail, Athens, c 159-138 BC; OPPOSITE TOP RIGHT: Van Pelt & Thompson, Gennadius Library, Athens, 1923-25; OPPOSITE BOTTOM: D Porphyrios, Pavilions at Highgate, London, 1981

This way the work of art may exist as a bridge between the example and the precept. It represents a universal truth (*ta katholu*/τά καθόλου) by imitating particular examples chosen for their typicality (*ta kath' ekaston*/τά καθ' ἔκαστον). This is not to say that a general idea is embodied in a particular example, but rather that the particular case is generalised by artistic treatment. No doubt this is what Goethe meant when he wrote that 'a special case requires nothing but the treatment of a poet to become universal'.

To return to architecture we might ask similarly of the way in which particular cases are generalised. The classical architrave generalises the otherwise particular and contingent experience of post-and-lintel construction. The aim here is not to reproduce the lintel itself as a structural member, with its sectional dimensions and material properties specified by the engineer, for that would be a symbolically mute gesture. Instead, the form of the classical architrave makes us see the structural members which produced it in the first place, from which it has detached itself as art, and to which it always alludes. The form of the classical architrave makes us recognise the universal law of gravity and stability. Recognition, here, is the experience of familiarity with the world not simply as a collection of contingent objects and events but as an intelligible narrative. Nobody would dispute that such narratives are ideologically produced and sanctioned through the employment of values, beliefs and myths. But *mythos* is not a dirty word as contemporary post-structuralists would have it. On the contrary, 'the reason why men enjoy seeing a likeness', writes Aristotle, 'is that in contemplating it they find themselves learning or inferring and saying perhaps, "Ah, that is he".' It is this emotional delight accompanying the pleasure of recognition of what is true *for us* that becomes the chief factor in the enjoyment of the arts. The theory of imitation (*mimesis*) seems to suggest, therefore, that art and architecture is a form of knowledge that serves to deepen our understanding of ourselves and thus our familiarity with the world.

I must side-step here for a moment and say something in response to the recent criticism of the aesthetics of imitation. Imitation, the recent deconstructionists have argued, is essentially dependent on *doxa* (δόξα), that is, on 'points of view'. Such points of view ultimately converge in common sense, formulate social identities and become, thereby, prejudiced 'plots' of legitimation.

The realisation that art is always ideological is no news; Marx and Nietzsche have argued this point convincingly. What the deconstructionists underestimate, however, is that this point of view of ideology is the only access we have to social life. Without our own points of view the world around us would be unintelligible. It is one thing to criticise those who boast that their point of view is uniquely privileged and another to conclude that no point of view can ever be taken on account of a paranoia of closure. At any rate, I know of no real achievement (I am speaking of the world of art) that was not based on *some* point of view. 'Is this a failing? And even if it were, why is this failure always present when anything is achieved?' (Gadamer). Again and again we find that art does more than engage us in an

ABOVE: *Trajaneum, Acropolis of Pergamum, c 125 AD; OPPOSITE TOP LEFT: Hall of Tuthmosis at the Temple of Amon-Ra, Karnak, c 1460 BC; OPPOSITE TOP RIGHT: Temple of Hadrian, Ephesus c 117-138 AD; OPPOSITE BOTTOM: Palace of Knossos, Crete, c 1600 BC, reconstructed by Sir Arthur Evans, c 1900-32*

ideological debate. Art takes the points of view (*doxa*) of everyday life and gives us back fictional narratives (*mythos*) which have a cognitive role in social life. In other words, art questions the very assumptions of ideology by recognising both its necessity and its pretensions. That is why art has more to do with freedom than with dogma. That is the sense in which we can say that art tells the 'truth' and never conspires to deceive.

*　　　*　　　*

At this point it may be useful to state in summary some of the main ideas I hope to have elicited from my exercise on Aristotle's *Poetics* as pertaining to mimesis. First, artistic imitation does not refer to the servile duplication of the model; it is neither a copy nor a simulation that aims at deception. Instead, art imitates by offering sensuous representations of the world so that we may come closer to knowing it. Secondly, there is the matter of what art imitates: '. . . reality past or present; things as they are said or seem to be; or things as they ought to be.' In all cases the artist imitates what he has deemed relevant for representation. Thirdly, there is a sense of 'truth' in all artistic imitation. The artist imitates no physical objects as such but rather 'things' (that is, matters of pertinence) in so far as they have a significance for him. In that sense, artistic imitation discloses the way in which the world is true *for us*. Fourthly, there is the question of likeness in all representation. Likeness here must be understood in three ways. Initially, when we say that a work of art is a likeness of some-'thing' we imply that we expect of art to use sensuous images as its medium rather than intellectual or discursive language. At the same time we feel that a work of art is a likeness only when it is rendered in a medium that is materially different from that in which the model is fashioned in the first place. This requirement introduces a necessary and telling distance from the model. In fact, the experience of art itself lies exactly in the nature of this distance. That is why the fiction of art does *not* conspire to deceive. Instead, the 'lies' of art speak of truth. Art imitates particular examples from the world, turns them into mythical fictions and makes them speak of universal truth.

Finally, the aim (purpose) of imitation in art is to afford an emotional delight that accompanies the pleasure of recognition of what is true *for us*. The artist shows us in sensuous form a representation of some-'thing'. This image-making always involves establishing a distance from the model. It is exactly this distance which gives significance and truth to the work of art. It is the distance that separates the timber shed from the temple that gives classical architecture its significance as a commemoration of shelter, construction and the laws of nature. It is the distance which separates the real cow from that painted by Van Doesburg that makes the painting a canonic statement of the primacy of objective, abstract essences. The Aristotelian theory of imitation (*mimesis*) is at the core of both traditional and modernist art.

The subject of imitation raises the question of how art and architecture can be meaningful. Architecture as one of the aspects of civilisation is

ABOVE: Michelangelo, Porta Pia, Rome, c 1561-65; OPPOSITE TOP LEFT: House in Ubeda, Spain, c 1550; OPPOSITE TOP RIGHT: Seville Cathedral, side entry, c 15th century; OPPOSITE BOTTOM: House on the fortified walls of Castiglion Fiorentino, Tuscany

concerned with images which afford recognition of the world. The roof, the truss, the portico, the column, the ochre or white-washed wall, the brick pergola opening up to the garden, all connect one building with another and help make intelligible our architectural experience of the world. Through the fictional images of imitation architecture raises itself above the mere contingencies of building and sets symbols for recognition. These symbols are composed, varied and re-composed in an ever-changing chain of transformations. Yet always the aim is to make man come to terms with the world.

If we take these observations into account, it will appear that raising the question of imitation in art and architecture is to begin to elicit that which is lasting and true for us from the transient.

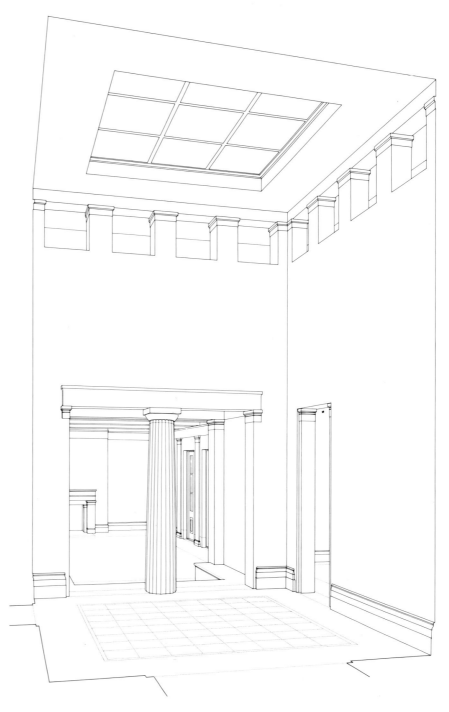

RIGHT: D Porphyrios, House in Athens, central atrium, 1990; OPPOSITE: The Arch of Hadrian, Athens, c 131-132 AD

CHAPTER II
FROM *TECHNE* TO TECTONICS

'Tectonics . . . envelop the bare form of construction with a symbolism of order.'
Karl Bötticher, Die Tektonik der Hellenen

'The roof must no longer support a load but only be supported, and this character
of not supporting must be visible on itself: it must be so constructed that it cannot
support anything and must therefore terminate at an angle.'
G W F Hegel, Aesthetics

We all know from our experience that the craft of making a chair or a table is very different from the fine arts, say, of sculpture or painting. And yet, on closer examination, we find the same procedure in the activity of the cabinet maker and the sculptor or of the weaver and the painter. The making of a utensil or tool and the making of a statue both require craftsmanship. In fact, craftsmen and artists alike have always valued very highly the mastery of their craft.

It should not surprise us, therefore, that the Greeks, who gave a lot of attention and thought to their works of art, used the same word for both art and craft, namely *techne* ($\tau\acute{\epsilon}\chi\nu\eta$). Craftsmen and artists alike were all thought of as *technites* ($\tau\epsilon\chi\nu\acute{\iota}\tau\epsilon\varsigma$), that is men who had a *techne* and knew how to practice it. And yet, in sharp contrast to Greek practice, our everyday experience tells us that there is a difference between craft and art. In these circumstances we must not hastily dismiss either our everyday experience or that of the ancients but we must rather consider further the meaning of the concept of *techne*.

In Greek, *techne* refers neither to craft nor to art and it does not have the sense of the technical or of technique as we may otherwise assume. In other words, it does not refer merely to a kind of practical facility in performance or dexterity in execution. Quintilian makes this point clear when he recounts that of all Hellenistic painters, Antiphilos was the most accomplished in 'ease of execution', or *facilitas*, translating in this manner the Greek term *hexis* ($\acute{\epsilon}\xi\iota\varsigma$), which means a trained skill. But such mere skill in draughts-manship does not comprise the *techne*, say, of painting.

Instead, the Greek word *techne* refers to a kind of knowledge. It implies method and consistency and it represents man's reasoned intelligence put into practice. *Techne* is an ordered application of knowledge that is intended to produce a specific product, or achieve a predetermined goal. Formerly, the various kinds of work demanding special skill and knowledge were

OPPOSITE: Stoa of Attalos, Athens, c 159-138 BC,
reconstructed by J Travlos, 1953-56

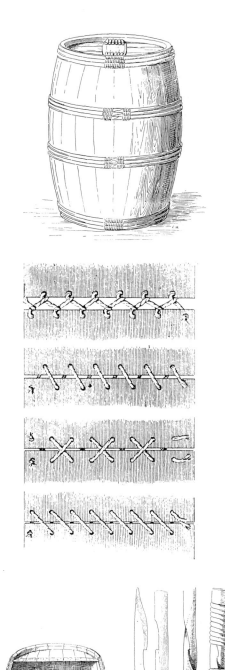

ABOVE TOP, MIDDLE & BOTTOM, AND OPPO-SITE TOP LEFT & MIDDLE LEFT: The stylised bands which adorn many clay vases are symbolic allusions to early forms of the stitched seam and the rope, after C Uhde, Die Konstructionen und die Kunstformen Architektur, *1903; OPPOSITE TOP RIGHT: A volcanic island has a definite but intel-ligible form; OPPOSITE MIDDLE RIGHT: The form of an automobile speaks of its intended use; OPPO-SITE BOTTOM LEFT & RIGHT: Plaited wickerwork and wattling as an early form of construction and building, after C Uhde*

covered by this word *techne* and the Greeks applied the term equally to agriculture, medicine, carpentry, pottery, engraving, as well as to painting, sculpture, architecture, music and poetry. This essential meaning of *techne* as reasoned intelligence and knowledge put into practice can be also found in the old German *kunst* or the Swedish *konst* which today stand for art but which originally meant knowledge and skill deriving from the root word *kennen* or *können*, to know, with the sense of a know-how.

Perhaps the most overriding characteristic of this classical concept is that *techne* is frequently opposed to nature (*physis*). In Greek thought it is gen-erally assumed that whereas nature acts out of sheer necessity, *techne* involves a deliberate human intention, a procedure of deliberately achieving a preconceived goal by means of reasoned intelligence and skill. But in order to be purposeful *techne* must follow rational rules. The system of such rules, or the organised body of knowledge related to some kind of production, is an essential part of *techne*. In his *Nicomachean Ethics* Aris-totle speaks of *techne* as 'a productive capacity involving a true course of reasoning'. This reasoned intelligence exhibited by a *techne* implies that it is possible to formulate the theory of its practice and it is this theory which constitutes a form of knowledge that becomes its distinguishing feature.

Craft, in this sense, is a *techne* in as much as it takes raw nature and transforms it into useful utensils and tools by means of a carefully preconceived and reasoned intelligence. A volcanic island by contrast is something material that has a definite but unintelligible form. What I mean here is that though the volcanic rock might have a shape and form, it nonetheless reveals nothing of the way in which it was made. Even if we were knowledgeable mineralogists the best we could do is give an explanation of its volcanic formation but we could offer no explanation of the ultimate purpose of its existence. From this point of view, the volcanic rock is a product of nature in that it has not been intended.

But a coffee pot, an axe, or an automobile exhibit a selection of matter and form that is guided by the respective purpose and usefulness of the artefact. It is in this sense that we say that the utensil or tool is well made, for it fulfils its goal when it is used. Its purpose is to be used in the way which was intended in the first place. It would be ludicrous to claim that a shoe could be worn as a glove or, for that matter, that walls could be horizontal and floors vertical. The utensil or tool as the product of craft fulfils its purpose only when it is used. Once it is no longer useful, either due to failure or obsolescence, it is mute and quite often its form becomes unintelligible. How many times have we not found ourselves staring at some bygone tool or instrument in a museum, struggling to decipher its intended use? But as long as the utensil or tool, as the product of a craft, is still useful and is being used (such as a barrel, for example, that is soundly made and will not disintegrate under the pressure of the liquid contained) then its form, which was the outcome of pure necessity and usefulness in the first place, now becomes a *typical* form. In other words, it becomes a form by which the intended use is recognised. Similarly the rope, the plaited band or the wicker basket have forms which point to their usefulness, while showing explicitly the *techne*

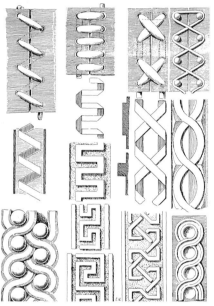

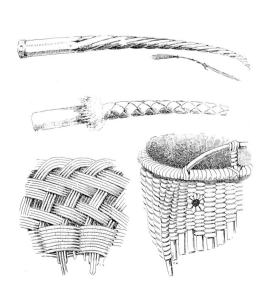

that guided their making. In fact, on certain occasions, utensils made by craftsmen exclusively for practical use transcend their purpose as useful objects and acquire, through their familiar form, the status of a symbol.

How is this possible and what do we mean here by the word 'symbol'? Originally in Greek it stood for a mark or a token, an outward sign through which the host could recognise his visitors and guests. Symbols were the broken pieces of a plate or an urn that the host gave to his guests as mementoes. Once these symbols were pieced together the whole could be reconstructed in an act of acknowledgement or recognition. The symbol (from the Greek *symballein*, συμβάλλειν, to put together) takes form, therefore, far from its origins in usefulness and into the realm of uselessness. This is a uselessness, however, which serves to celebrate remembrance by means of convention.

The stylised bands which adorn many clay vases are but symbolic allusions to the early forms of the stitched seam and the rope. Although this decorative adornment is useless, it is nonetheless highly pleasurable for it makes us relate back to an anterior mode of construction; be that of the flask with its seams binding the hide or of the barrel tied together by wicker ropes. When habitually encoded, such symbols become accepted decorative motifs that afford recognition of man as *homo faber*. The artist is a *technites* not because he is a craftsman who works with his hands, but because he possesses the knowledge and skill that serve to deepen our understanding of ourselves as makers, as *homo faber*, and thus our familiarity with the world.

*   *   *

Keeping in mind these observations, let us now consider the case of what 'building' means. Words for 'building' are in part connected with verbs for 'dwell' through the notion of remaining in a place. Heidegger's seminal essay 'Building, Dwelling, Thinking' lovingly argued this case.

The Old English and High German word for building, *büan*, means to dwell on and till the land. The same idea is found in the Dutch *bouwen* and the Danish *bygge* or Swedish *bygga*, which mean to settle. Heidegger, to his credit, was the first to explore this existential meaning of building as dwelling. But at the same time he appears to have suppressed (for reasons which must be the subject of another study) a whole other group of words for building which reflect the activity, skill or knowledge of constructing.

Whereas the Old English and High German word *büan*, to build, means to dwell, the Greek word *oekodomeo*, (οἰκοδομέω), 'to build', derives from *oekos*, meaning house or dwelling, and the root of the verb *demo* (δέμω), meaning to tie and put together, to construct. What is so significant about this? Fundamentally that the Greek word *oekodomeo* distinguishes between the act of dwelling (as in *oekos*), and the act of constructing a dwelling. In fact this sense of putting together and constructing of the Greek *demo* is so strong that it gives rise to an alternative word for house, namely *domos* (δόμος). Thus in Greek there are two words for house: *Oekos*, from the verb *oeko*, to dwell, which stresses the sense of house as dwelling, and *domos*, from the verb *demo*,

ABOVE: Trajan's Kiosk, Island of Philae, c 96 AD; OPPOSITE TOP: KF Schinkel, Altes Museum, Berlin, 1823-30; OPPOSITE BOTTOM: A Aalto, The sauna of Villa Mairea, Noormarkku, 1937-38

to construct, which highlights the sense of house as a constructed entity.

This archaeology of language becomes even more fascinating when one probes further into the original meaning of the verb *demo*, to construct, for it appears that it derives from the sanskrit *dama* and the Indo-European root *dem*, which mean 'to build' but formerly also carried the meaning of 'joining and fitting together'. In this sense the Greek word *oekodomeo*, to build, points to a specific mode of making one's house, namely that of joining and fitting together the pieces that will make a place for dwelling.

This emphasis on the particular method of constructing one's house is not found simply in the Greek *oekodomeo* but also in the language of other cultures that had much to do with the *techne* of building. Thus the Latin *aedificare*, to build, derives from *aedes*, house or temple, and the verb *facere*, to make. But we should not forget that *facere* does not generally mean 'to make' but indicates a specific manner of making, namely that of fashioning and moulding, as in the Latin *fingera*. In this sense the Latin *aedificare*, to build, points to a specific mode of making one's house, namely that of moulding the clay by hand.

Similarly, the French *bâtir* and Old French *bastir*, to build, derive from the Old High German word *bestan*, to bind. Building in the sense of binding, however, is still further qualified when we probe into the root of the word *bestan*, which comes from *bast*, referring to the inner bark of trees frequently used for plaiting wickerwork. In this sense the French word *bâtir*, to build, also points to a specific mode of building, that of binding together by plaiting. The same is true of the Welsh *adeilad*, to build, which derives from the root *ail* and literally means plaited work and wattling – the structure of interwoven sticks and twigs used for fences and walls. This latter sense of building suits, of course, the historical description of the hut of Romulus on the Forum in Rome and a similar hut on the Aeropagus in Athens, both referred to by Vitruvius.

I do not want you to think, however, that I am trying to prove by means of linguistics that the origins of building lie in the rustic hut. This was debated so thoroughly by the *Querelle* that I doubt that those who are still undecided will ever make up their minds. Instead, my interest here is to probe into the essential meaning of building as constructing and thereby come closer to the *techne*, that is to the body of knowledge, which was formerly required for building.

Originally the builder was a builder in timber – a carpenter – and only later was he to become a builder in stone or a mason. This is well illustrated by the Greek word for builder, *tecton* (τέκτων) from which tectonics, and eventually architecture, derive their meaning within the context of Western civilisation. The *tecton* was first of all an artisan in wood – a carpenter. In Plutarch *tecton* means carpenter and Thucydides distinguishes between *tectones* (carpenters) and *lithourgoi* (masons). This meaning of *tecton* as carpenter is found as late as in the New Testament where Matthew refers to Christ as *o tou tektonos yios* (ὁ τοῦ τέκτονος υἱός), the son of a carpenter.

If the builder, therefore, as *tecton*, is primarily a carpenter and only by later extension an artisan working in metal, stone, clay, paint, etc, his *techne*

ABOVE: Barn at Williamsburg, Virginia; OPPO-SITE: Celsus Library, Ephesus, c 115 AD, recon-structed by F Hueber, 1972-78

– that is the organised body of knowledge related to his production – is surely superseded by *tectonike*, carpentry, from which the word tectonics derives. In its original Greek sense the term tectonics, *tectonike*, describes the knowledge of carpentry.

But what are we to make of this? Surely it could not be that all building is carpentry nor that we ought to trace all buildings back to their original timber ancestors. In any event, even if we had the patience to compile an exhaustive list of the comparative genealogy of all building elements, the best we could hope to prove is that all building derives from carpentry.

However, this is not the significant point in the meaning of *tectonike* as the *techne* of carpentry. Much more essential is the realisation that tectonics invoke a potential order which is defined by the form-giving capacity of the material used. Thus in carpentry, timber as matter is not shapeless but is suggestive of form. At the same time timber has a finite length and width and therefore invites the artisan to treat construction in a dimensional and scalar sense. In addition, timber is discontinuous and so it begs the skill and knowledge of jointing.

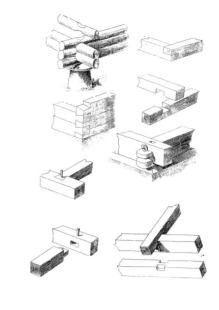

Tectonics, as the *techne* of carpentry, while speaking of the particular skill and knowledge of timber construction, at the same time delineates the ontological experience of construction. The concern of tectonics is threefold. First, the finite nature and formal properties of constructional materials, be those timber, brick, stone, steel, etc. Second, the procedures of jointing, which is the way that elements of construction are put together. Thirdly, the visual statics of form, that is the way by which the eye is satisfied about stability, unity and balance and their variations or opposites.

This means that in any encounter with building it is *not* the particular exigencies of construction, but rather, the ontological experience of tectonics that is brought to bear. *Tectonike* stands as the highest fulfilment of all construction. It makes construction speak out in the sense of revealing the ontology of constructing. For this reason it seems to me that any aesthetic theory which interprets tectonics simply as a set of signifying gestures added onto everyday practices of construction is thoroughly misleading. In some instances, this may well be the case (as for example, with the theory of the decorated shed adopted by Post-Modern Classicism and Post-Modern Modernism) and yet a few pilasters or some riveted joints thrown in as referential signs of a constructional order are not enough to give a building a tectonic presence.

Whenever we feel something is lacking in a building it is because it does *not* hang together. It is because we feel that there is no sense of the necessary, no sense of something that needs to be said and can only be said in that way. A tectonic experience, however, conveys both a sense of the necessary and freedom. It conveys a sense of the necessary because order is delimited by the form-giving capacity of the materials used. The form, say, of a panelled door speaks of its constructional assembly. The forms of the voussoir or the corbel are bound to a sense of necessary structural behaviour. The consistency, say, of roofing materials one finds in most vernacular towns derives from the exclusive use of indigenous materials and, by

ABOVE TOP: Timber jointing, after C Uhde; ABOVE MIDDLE: Window of Ionian House, after Viollet-le-Duc, Histoire de l'habitation humaine, 1876; ABOVE BOTTOM: Farm house in Mazandaran, Iran, after J Durm, Handbuch der Architektur, 1887; OPPOSITE TOP: Demetri Porphyrios, model of Propylon, Surrey, 1985; OPPOSITE BOTTOM LEFT: Traditional ashlar construction; OPPOSITE BOTTOM RIGHT: Post-Modernist construction of the decorated shed; OPPOSITE BOTTOM MIDDLE: Otto Wagner, Post-and-bracket detail, Majolica House, Vienna, c 1898

extension, from the absence of 'options'. In these and all similar cases, building technology is concerned with the useful and the necessary. Technology and tectonics here become synonymous, for there is no interest in mere gadgetry. The sham experience of gadgetry appears only when a contradiction is inserted between form and the necessary in the name of ostentation or as a sales incentive. Instead, the sense of the necessary and the inevitable that a tectonic experience conveys always derives from the construction, structure, or the materials used for shelter.

At the same time a tectonic experience conveys a sense of freedom. What I mean here is better understood using an analogy with play. We are familiar with play as being outside ordinary or 'real' life. Much the same way, tectonic order is a stepping out of 'real' construction and shelter. Much like play, tectonic order pretends it constructs shelter. Standing outside the realm of the necessary, it does *not* have to satisfy the engineer's calculations nor the performance requirements of the building trade. Yet, it sets its own rules as an image and make believe of real construction and shelter.

Once the rules of tectonics are set up, they become a treasure to be retained in memory and transmitted. We speak, therefore, of the traditions say of Classical, Gothic, Chinese, or Romanesque tectonics. And as is the case with all artistic fictions, tectonic fiction creates its own supreme order where the least deviation 'spoils the game'. Consider the analogy with, say, chess. We play a game of chess not out of necessity but of our own free will. And yet we are expected to follow the rules of the game which, in fact, have *not* been laid down by us. It would be absurd to claim that there should be three knights or two queens; not because the claim would contradict any pragmatic fact or necessity but simply because such a claim falls outside the rules of chess. In fact, such rules are never experienced as a constraint but rather as a mutually acceptable ordering framework within which we can exhibit our ingenuity as chess players.

This profound affinity between play and order is what makes the analogy with tectonics plausible. Tectonic order is indeed a fiction removed from the contingencies of construction and shelter, yet invested with the experience of stability, unity and balance which construction and shelter describe in the first place. The rules of a tectonic order are binding. 'No scepticism is possible', wrote Paul Valéry, 'where the rules of play are concerned for they are unshakable truths.' He who might wish to rob tectonic order of its rules is a spoil-sport.

We have now come full circle. Whenever we admire a building it is because it conveys both a sense of the necessary and freedom. It conveys a sense of the necessary because order is delimited by the form-giving capacity of the materials used; and a sense of freedom because it is bound by rules which are made as tokens of recognition of ourselves as *homo-faber*. This is what classical antiquity taught and it is precisely this that we seem to have forgotten.

ABOVE: D Porphyrios, House in Chelsea Square, London, 1990, (painting by Rita Wolff); OPPOSITE TOP: House in Cairo, timber rafters at eaves and projecting balcony; OPPOSITE BOTTOM: The dentils supporting the classical cornice represent the timber rafters of vernacular eaves construction

CHAPTER III

THE CLASSICAL ORDER

'And thus began . . . the tendency to turn into an image everything that delighted or troubled me and to come to some certain understanding with myself upon it, that I might both rectify my conceptions of external things, and set my mind at rest about them.'
J W Goethe, Dichtung und Wahrheit

'In mythical thought and imagination we do not meet with individual confessions. Myth is an objectification of man's social experience, not of his individual experience.'
Ernst Cassirer, The Myth of the State

We may regard architecture as the focal point of our everyday activities, but when we are asked to specify what architecture is, we immediately become confused. And yet we all seem to agree on one point at least, namely, that there is a distinction between building and architecture. Building, the Greek *oekodomike* (οἰκοδομική) as we have seen, refers to the *techne* of constructing shelter. It denotes the material techniques and body of knowledge surrounding construction, services, structure and functional disposition. Architecture, on the other hand, in the everyday use of the word, refers to the art of building, *l'art de bâtir*. Architecture appears to be the product of an artistic intention, whereas building is the product of necessity. Nevertheless, we feel that architecture is not merely a supplement to building, but that building and architecture are interrelated experiences, one focusing on the experience of craft, the other on the experience of art.

But what do we really mean when we say that architecture is an art? And further, what do we mean when we say that architecture is the 'art of building'?

The conception of architecture (and art in general) as having a relationship to contingent reality that is not direct but potential can be traced back to Greek antiquity. In his *Poetics*, Aristotle discusses poetry and art as a form of truth liberated from experience: a response awakened in the observer by the transformation of experience and contingent reality into fictitious play. The central principle of Aristotelian aesthetics is that art is the imitation of nature. We have already discussed in detail the meaning of Aristotelian *mimesis*. I have stressed that imitation does not denote the servile duplication of the model; it is neither a copy nor a simulation of the physical world that surrounds us. Art imitates nature in the sense that it fashions a likeness,

OPPOSITE: The Athenian Treasury, Delphi, c 507 BC

homeioma (ὁμοίωμα), of some-'thing' found in the world and in doing so it brings forward the essential significance that this some-'thing' has for us. Artistic imitation discloses the way by which the world is true for us.

But what is the nature of this *likeness* that art presents to us? Aristotle reminds us that the joy in the likeness or image which artistic imitation gives us is in fact the joy of recognition. Children enjoy doing this sort of thing. Consider how much pleasure they take in dressing up; and think of how annoyed they are when we fail to take their disguise seriously, for we are supposed to recognise who they are imitating. This is the motivation behind all mimetic forms of representation.

To *recognise* here, means something more than merely seeing something that we already know. The joy of recognition is rather that *more* becomes known than is already known. Recognition (*anagnorisis*, ἀναγνώρισις) in general and artistic recognition in particular always implies that we have come to know something more authentically than was possible when we were caught up in our everyday contingent encounter with it. In this sense the recognition that comes from artistic imitation elicits the permanent from the transient.

Turning now to the various arts, we see that each one of them imitates reality with a limited range of means, materials and techniques. Painting imitates reality by means of line and colour; sculpture by means of relief; music by means of sound; and poetry by means of language. Of course, there may be some overlap between the various arts, but what I wish to emphasise here is the essential, specific difference deriving from the medium of execution. A poem could be read aloud but that does not mean that its characteristic medium is sound; a statue may use polychromy but that does not make it a painting. From this point of view the various arts are but so many different 'imitations' of reality: each one makes its claim to truth with the tools and medium it knows best.

This emphasis on the autonomy of the individual arts was discussed extensively by Quatremère de Quincy and derives ultimately from Lessing's *Laocoön* or the *Limits of Painting and Poetry*, where he expounds on the idea of the artistic medium. Lessing, as we know, took issue with Winckelman, who ignored the differences between painting and sculpture by following the precept *Ut Pictura Poesis* ('as is painting so is poetry'). The formulation *ut pictura poesis* which is originally attributed to Horace, had become one of the commonplaces of aesthetics for centuries, enjoying great popularity during the Renaissance up until the middle of the eighteenth century. Lessing precisely criticised this claim of similarity among the arts. Instead, he stressed that each of the arts follows its own rules and that its artistic medium delimits boundaries which cannot be transgressed.

I am aware of the recent Post-Modernist debate as regards exactly this very issue of the autonomy versus dispersion of the various arts. The advent of deconstructive readings, however, cannot possibly lessen the wisdom of the ancients. Not only does deconstruction presuppose construction (and is therefore intelligible only by reference to a specific set of norms); it itself establishes new rules from the ruins of what it demolishes.

The notion of the autonomy of each of the arts, therefore, recoils back at

ABOVE: Agesander, Athenodorus and Polydorus of Rhodes, The Laocoön Group, late 2nd century BC, Vatican Museum, Rome; OPPOSITE: Mnesicles and Callimachus (?), The Erechtheum, Athens, c 421-405 BC

us. The various arts are but so many different 'imitations' of reality: each one makes its claim to truth with the tools and medium it knows best. Then, I will ask, does this idea of autonomy apply equally to architecture? What are the means of architectural imitation and what is architecture supposed to imitate?

Let us return for a moment to that early, pre-architectural stage, when the only thing we had was the craft of building. Repetition and empirical judgement led builders to develop a habit of 'seeing' and 'judging' the constructional soundness and functional convenience of a particular solution. Over the centuries, a few chosen building solutions acquired a natural authority. Such is the power of habit and consensus that these soon became universal laws, shedding their marks of particularity and stressing their typicality (eg the idea of 'gable' as opposed to the gable of my house).

In contemplating these select forms, man recognises in them the cumulative knowledge and experience of his building *techne* and the genius of his species and thereby wishes to commemorate them. At that very moment, these forms lose their use value and assume a symbolic value. The necessities of construction and shelter are commemorated by means of symbolic form: building becomes architecture. 'It is not for pleasure but out of necessity that our temples have gables', Cicero wrote. 'The need for discharging rainwater has suggested their form. And yet, such is the beauty of their form . . . that if one were to build a temple on Mount Olympus – where I am told it never rains – one would still feel obliged to crown it with a pediment.'

Ethnologists have argued that, in the realm of technical achievement, as soon as man invents and employs a tool, he views it not as a mere artefact but as something endowed with powers of its own. The axe and the hammer seem to have attained such mythic significance in the earliest times, but the cult of other implements, such as the fishhook, the spear or the sword, may be found to this day among primitive peoples. Primitive man used image or picture magic with the aim of gaining power over the things and beings represented. Consider the dolls used for bewitching which are spoken of as early as in the ancient Chaldean incantations and survive even among the 'civilised' industrial nations of today in the burning of effigies at demonstrations.

I am bringing this up only because it could conceivably be argued that the pediment, for example, might have originally been a cult image. But whether the pediment, (or for that matter architectural forms in general), had a mythico-religious rather than commemorative origin does not affect my argument here. Hersey's claim, in his *Lost Meaning of Classical Architecture*, that the origins of Classical forms are to be found in an archaic state of terror does not preclude that such cultic symbols may not recur purged of their original dionysian horror. In fact, that was the very achievement of classical Greek culture: images which may have had their origins in archaic terror were now tamed as symbols of order in the idea of tectonics. What is significant in classical architecture is that the *techne* of construction and shelter is both the subject-matter and the means of its imitation.

ABOVE: Bodley and Garner, Longwall Quadrangle, Magdalen College, Oxford, c 1880s; OPPOSITE TOP & BOTTOM: Houses in Symi, c 1910

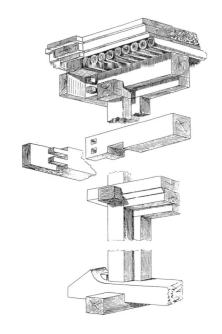

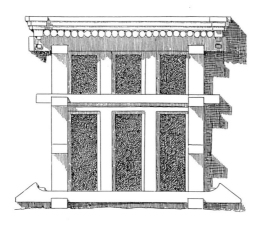

ABOVE & OPPOSITE LEFT: Architecture imitates construction and shelter by means of tectonics: Arsaces Tomb at Myra, timber construction; Arsaces Tomb at Myra, stone construction; Lomas Rishi cave imitating the contemporary timber chaityas, Behar, India, c 260 BC; Lykian Tomb in British Museum; section of stave church at Borgund; timber construction of Doric Temple, after C Uhde; OPPOSITE RIGHT: T Hansen, Athens Academy, detail of front portico, Athens, c 1859-87

It is in this sense that architecture is meant to imitate the *techne* of its building craft. The Greek word for architecture is *arche-tectonike* (ἀρχιτεκτονική). *Arche*, here, as always, signifies primacy either in a temporal sense, meaning beginning and origins, or in the sense of rank, implying power and dominion. Architecture, therefore, as *arche-tektonike*, denotes either the origins of building in tectonics (that is the *techne* of *tectonike*, carpentry) or the power and dominion of tectonics. Thus the etymology, historical development and formal preoccupation of architecture confirm that its aim is to imitate construction and shelter by means of *tectonic order*.

The Sumerian temple imitates the reed construction with which houses were built. The rock-cut tomb of Arsaces in Myra imitates the constructional principles of indigenous timber-framing. The Lykian tomb, now in the British Museum, is a representation in stone of the contemporary elements of building construction. The Indian Behar caves represent in the rock the timber construction of the contemporary chaityas. Two wooden posts sloping slightly inwards support longitudinal rafters morticed into their heads while smaller rafters on each side and at the top of an arcuated framework support the roof; the latter rendered in layers of thatch or plank with an ogee summit to form a watershed. Similarly, the partially engaged columns that subdivide a wall in early Romanesque architecture do not derive from classical antiquity, as is wrongly assumed by many historians, but formalise in stone the round timber pales used in the construction of Norwegian stave churches, as at Borgund. Finally, the applied order of the portico in the Forum Holitorium in Rome shows the way in which Hellenistic and Roman architecture celebrate the constructional principles of both post-and-lintel and arcuated tectonics.

This list is only indicative, but one could draw examples from primitive architecture, the architecture of early civilisations, of the Far East or of our own Western tradition.

Of the various architectures that have flourished over the ages, the architecture of Greek antiquity best exemplifies the idea of tectonic order. Owing to their belief that the highest achievement of art was its ability to stand between the example and the precept, the Greeks managed to grasp clearly the relation between vernacular building and classical architecture.

Despite the superficial association with rusticity that the word vernacular carries, the emphasis I have in mind here is different. For essentially, vernacular does not refer to the primitivism of pre-industrial cultures, but to the ethos of straightforward construction, to the rudimentary building of shelter, an activity that exhibits a catholicity of reason, efficiency, economy, durability and pleasure. Certainly, variations in materials and techniques impart regionalist characteristics to vernacular buildings. Yet there are a number of constructional experiences which are universal and as such are grounded in the ontology of building as *tectonike*.

Consider the experiences of load-bearing and load-borne, as exemplified by the post-and-lintel, or the experience of horizontal and vertical enclosure, principally the roof and the wall. The floor, since it repeats the original ground, is flat, for it is meant to be walked upon; whereas the roof is inclined

since, in addition to shedding off water, it marks the terminus of the building and should appear as such. At the same time, and since all building (as *tectonike*) is construction by means of joining finite elements, the act of building necessarily involves the experience of demarcating, in the sense of defining the beginning and ending of the various constructional elements.

When applied to building, such universal constructional experiences give rise to syntactic and figurative images; as for example the gable, which marks the sectional termination of the roof and thus points to the primary experience of entry; or the engaged pilaster, which reveals the confluent experiences of load bearing and enclosure; or the window and door, which manifest the experience of suspending enclosure locally for purposes of passage; or the colonnade, which demarcates the experience of boundary. The trilithon of pre-historic times is the fundamental idea behind the principle of the post-and-lintel, for here we experience the conquest of man over earthbound matter. The trilithic construction of post-and-lintel stands between two worlds not only as partition, as is the case of the wall, but also as a connecting gate. In the image of the gate, vernacular building attempts to symbolise, for the first time, the idea of the house as shelter. The tiles or pediment stand for the roof, the architrave for both structure and enclosure, while the door denotes both passage and the security it guarantees when closed. No wonder that all civilisations have lavished such great attention on the design of their gates.

Yet architecture cannot remain at this 'starting point'. Its aim as art is to make us look at construction and shelter so that we may come to know the laws of nature more authentically than we could when caught up in our everyday contingent encounter with building. In that sense, classical architecture is not merely a second version or copy of building construction, but rather a recognition of the essential laws of nature which are now formalised in the sensuous medium of *tectonics*.

In the tectonics of classical architecture the experience of load-bearing is represented by the entasis of the column, while the primary experience of post-and-lintel construction is formalised in the architrave of Greek antiquity. The chief beam binding the columns together and imposing on them a common load becomes the architrave. The syncopation of the transversal beams resting on the architrave is represented by the triglyphs and metopes of the frieze. One recalls here the literary evidence of *Iphigenia in Tauris*, where Pylades advises Orestes that if he wants to get into the temple of Diana unnoticed, he should slip through the voids of the metopes. This shows clearly that the stone architecture of Greek antiquity imitated timber construction. Similarly, the projecting rafters of the roof which carry the gutter above the frieze are formalised in the idea of the cornice. The mutules, dentils, guttae, echinus, abacus, and so on, are all images that imitate their respective constructional models.

Most significantly, the whole tectonic assemblage of column, architrave, frieze and cornice becomes the ultimate object of classical contemplation in the idea of the Order. The Classical Order sets form over the necessities of shelter and tectonics over the contingencies of construction. It provides a

ABOVE: The trilithic construction of the Dolmen, Sealand, Denmark; OPPOSITE TOP LEFT: Ictinus and Callicrates, detail from the Parthenon, Athens, 447-438 BC; OPPOSITE TOP RIGHT: Mnesicles and Callimachus (?), detail from the Erechtheum, Athens, c 421-405 BC; OPPOSITE BOTTOM: Mnesicles, detail from the Propylaea, Athens, 437-432 BC

definitive account of the laws of nature as manifested through construction and shelter. Whereas the diversity of the contingent world is constantly on the verge of dissolution and the forms of the real world blossom and wilt, the Classical Order makes us see the immutable laws of nature by means of tectonic fiction.

That is what makes us call classical whatever is retrieved from the vicissitudes of changing time and changing taste. That is why the term classical always points to something enduring, with a significance that is independent of all circumstances of time. In those things we name classical we recognise a kind of timeless present that is contemporaneous and at ease with every historical period. That is why I have insisted on so many occasions on the rhetorical expression 'classicism is *not* a style'.

In the Classical Order the power of mythic fiction presides, becoming first the cultic and then the prime aesthetic subject-matter of Classical architecture. The Classical Order constructs a tectonic fiction out of the constructional necessities of building. The artifice of constructing this fictitious world is seen as analogous to the laws of nature and as a precept for constructing the human world. Myth allows for a convergence of the real and the fictive so that the real is redeemed.

But nature here must be understood as including human nature, for the Classical Order imitates human temperament and rank as well. The masculine, feminine and sophisticated temperaments of the Doric, Ionic and Corinthian Orders refer to the mythic experience of human ontology. Later, as the magic circle of mythical consciousness is broken, the Classical Orders assume an 'aesthetic' role and become rhetorical devices for establishing the decorum of social propriety.

Allow me here one final detour. The 'aesthetic' role of the Classical Orders has been often treated by historians and critics alike as 'a fall from grace'. It has been argued that once the Orders lost their cultic significance they assumed a mere 'decorative' function. This passage from cultic veneration to the aesthetics of decorum inevitably undermined their credibility, so the argument continues, relegating their forms to arbitrary and, therefore, dispensable ornament.

We must ask, however, a more essential question: could it be that order and ornament are related? Language, here, shows us the way. In Greek, order and decoration derive from a similar experience. As it appears in Homer, *kosmein* (κοσμεῖν), to decorate, initially meant to 'bring to order' and regulate as in the order in which rowers sit, the order of the combatants in battle and most significantly the civic order which binds the citizens. The expression *kata kosmon* (κατά κόσμον), according to the right order, was meant to suggest the idea of propriety and of the befitting. It was in this sense that *kosmos* (κόσμος) was eventually linked to adornment. In fact, even today the Greek *kosmos* refers both to order and adornment and, by extension, it also takes the sense of the human world in general, or even still of the order of the universe as in the English derivative of 'cosmic' order.

ABOVE: Byzantine Church of the Apostles, Athens, c 1020; OPPOSITE: Abd Al-Rahman Mosque, Cordoba, end of 8th century

In this context the Classical Orders stand as the grand metaphor of the tectonic order of the world, and as such they become the most appropriate

kosmema (κόσμημα), or ornament. We should not hurriedly dismiss the sense that this linguistic doubling entails: to ornament, from the Latin *ornare*, means literally 'to put in order'. Such is the essential object of the aesthetics of decorum. But I should leave this subject for further elaboration in the next chapter.

*　　*　　*

I began by considering the way in which building is at the root of all architectural imitation by being both the subject-matter of architecture and its means of imitation. Constructional technique and the commodious disposition of shelter are the starting points. Sound building shows the way to typical solutions. The formal characteristics of these solutions acquire a symbolic value over the years. In a long process of stylisation and refinement, these symbolic forms are gradually objectified in their typicality. Architecture is born! Architecture imitates its own origins in its past as building and throughout a process of mythical animation it assigns to all time-honoured building solutions a special tectonic form. The Classical Orders, by means of tectonic order, celebrate the laws of both physical and human nature.

In this sense Classical architecture – and by extension, traditional architecture in general – is neither an arbitrary adornment of building nor the inevitable causal outcome of building technique. Rather it is the symbolic form that man gives to his building craft when he imitates such craft by means of tectonics. That is why architecture makes us see the building craft from which it is born, from which it detaches itself as art, and to which it always alludes.

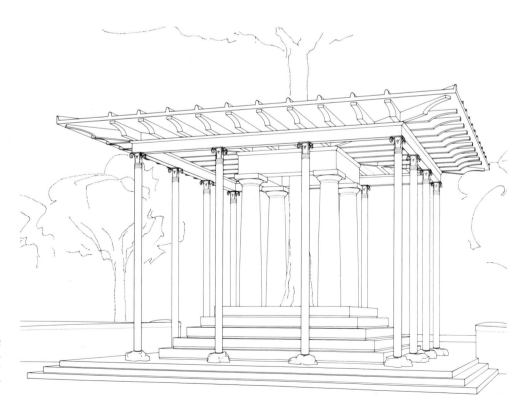

RIGHT: D Porphyrios, Pavilion in Battery Park City, New York, 1989; OPPOSITE TOP: A Palladio, Villa Almerico, (Rotonda), Vicenza, c 1570; OPPOSITE BOTTOM: A Palladio, Villa Emo, Fanzolo, (Treviso), c 1561-64

CHAPTER IV
CHARACTER AND STYLE

'The products of art require the pre-existence of an efficient precedent similar to themselves; as for example with the art of sculpture, which must necessarily precede this specific statue for the latter cannot be produced spontaneously.'
Aristotle, De partibus animalium

'We are ready for all the joys of exploring our own freedom; infinity is open to us. Yes, but that can induce vertigo!'
Le Corbusier, The Decorative Art of Today

Quite often we describe buildings as if they had a personality: they can be elegant or heavy, forthcoming or withdrawn. When such a personality is felt to be the voice of the architect himself, we call it style: *le style, c'est l'homme*. This conception of style as the distinctive signature of the artist is based on the assumption that every artist has his own imagery, his own preoccupations and his own formal conventions. Thus understood, style had its great period in late Victorian times when the primary connection between artistic form and personality was a fundamental artistic value and a principle of criticism.

Classical thought, however, has taken a very different view. Plato, who seems to have been fascinated by the visual arts, nevertheless considered artistic production a mere falsification of reality. In an often quoted passage from the *Republic*, Plato tells us that in contrast to the carpenter who, in constructing a couch, imitates the idea of the couch in the form of a concrete and useful artefact, the painter merely reproduces an illusion of the carpenter's couch which is twice removed from the 'truth of the idea'. Art is, in fact, a trivial pursuit since it offers no cognitive value, and artistic invention is but the fanciful conjecture of divine madness built on nothing firm. But while the notion of artistic invention as madness has been previously advanced in order to arrogate a privileged status to the poet, Plato managed to trivialise art by giving it the rather unrespectable sense of an obstacle in the way of true knowledge.

Later, in contrast to Plato, Aristotle stressed that artistic production is linked to man's practical and inventive intelligence. In his *Metaphysics*, Aristotle distinguishes three aspects of the production process: every object is formed by an 'agency'; it is formed 'from something'; and it is formed 'into something'. Art, therefore, much like medicine or carpentry, is a rational productive activity. Men take a natural pleasure in art since the experience

OPPOSITE: Friedrich von Gärtner, Old Palace, Athens, c 1837-41

of art entails a process of understanding and learning. Aristotle restores to the artist something of the knowledge and wisdom which Greek tradition had always claimed for him. However, it is not the personality of the artist that determines the work but rather the *techne*, as a body of knowledge, know-how and skill. What differs from one artist to another is the degree of knowledge and skill or *virtue* (ἀρετή); there is no indication of a personal style that transcends the knowledge of his *techne*.

The question of style, therefore, does *not* exist in classicism since the individual personality is always informed by the principles of the *techne*. 'The products of art', writes Aristotle in *De partibus animalium*, 'require the pre-existence of an efficient precedent similar to themselves; as for example with the art of sculpture, which must necessarily precede this specific statue, for the latter cannot be produced spontaneously.' The notion of the isolated individual genius and of his contempt for the guiding rules of *techne*, that we know from Romanticism, are alien to classical thought.

In these matters, the prevalent consideration of the classical tradition revolves around the theory of decorum. Decorum refers to that which is 'fitting'. In its Latin use decorum had the same sense of the proper, suitable, or seemly which it still carries in English. In architecture, decorum came to mean the appropriateness of form to the programme and to the physical or social context and circumstances. Hence the beauty arising from fitness. In this context, the romantic conception of style is of little use and, instead, we must turn to the classical concept of *character*.

Character, from the Greek χαρακτήρ, originally referred to the man who sharpened utensils and thus knew how to inscribe on wood, stone or brass. At the time that minting began, this word lost its sense of *nomen agentis* and came to mean first an impression and then by extension a coin, stamp or seal. In the case of an authoritative mark, character would also refer to a sign, particularly a letter, as can still be seen today when we refer to the characters of the alphabet. The sense of an impression or of an image on a coin explains why character, in its early use, also denoted the typical features of a man. Herodotus speaks of Astyages recognising the young Cyrus by the character of his face (χαρακτήρ τοῦ προσώπου); and Theophrastus was the first to build up a kind of moral typology in his treatise entitled *Characters* of 319 BC.

The idea of character as a theoretical concept originally derives from Aristotle's theory of human nature. In his *Poetics*, Aristotle pointed out that all people are marked by specific physical and behavioural attributes. More importantly for Aristotle, character was an expression of moral purpose. It was only later, when Greco-Roman rhetoricians gave different literary treatment to their subjects in oratory, that character came to mean style, in the sense of personal expression. The classical idea of character, however, never stressed individual but always typical traits.

For the classical mind, everything in the world has a character of its own in the sense that it bears distinctive features by which we can recognise it. In a manner similar to nature, therefore, those artefacts made by the craftsman and artist must also be given their own distinctive character. Character here

ABOVE: Giovanni and Bartolomeo Buon, Doge's Palace, Venice, c 1309-1424; OPPOSITE: A Palladio, Palazzo Chiericati, detail of loggia, c 1550

is not meant to facilitate the recognition of the artist's hand; it is rather an attribute that assigns proper and typical features to artefacts, so they may speak of their purpose, rank, and immediate context or distant ancestors.

In the practice of classical workshops like those, for example, of the painter Parrhasius, the sculptor Polyclitus, or later in the Hellenistic period, the sculptor Xenocrates, specific rules were developed for giving character to artefacts. These rules, though specifically referring to painting and sculpture, were equally valid for architecture. They did not, however, spell out the particular technicalities necessary for the execution of a painting, statue or building. Instead they functioned as principles; or better still, they pointed out areas of formal concern for the artist. Character was given to an artefact by the combination of the following four considerations: *symmetria*, *rhythm*, *akribeia*, and *ornament*. I will briefly touch upon the meaning of the first three and then dwell in more detail on the significance of ornament.

In the later part of the fifth century BC, the sculptor Polyclitus wrote a theoretical treatise that must have enjoyed great prestige and popularity in the classical world. The *Canon* of Polyclitus, as it was called, has not survived but we know of it and of its contents from a passage in a treatise by Galen of Pergamon, the consultant physician to Marcus Aurelius, who lived in the second century AD. Though many centuries had passed since the time of Polyclitus, the teachings of his *Canon* were still in use.

Contrary to modern experience, we should not be surprised to find a physician commenting on proportion and beauty. In classical antiquity, medicine was one of the arts (a *techne*) in as much as the physician, by imitating nature's healing processes, extended the work of nature. In keeping with classical practice, Galen believed that beauty did not refer to some particular substance lodged in an object but rather to the balanced relationship between the parts and the whole. We thus have Galen's own testimony of 'one finger to another, and of all the fingers to the wrist and the forearm, and of the forearm to the arm, in fact of all parts to everything, as is written in the *Canon* of Polyclitus. For having taught us in that treatise all the *symmetriae* of the human body, Polyclitus supported his treatise with a model statue of a man made in accordance with the principles of his treatise, which statue, like the treatise, he called the *Canon*.'

We should not think of the treatise, however, as a workshop manual in the sense of a practical recipe book. Instead it provided rules of anthropometry with the emphasis always on the relational aspects of measure. *Symmetria* (συμμετρία) has nothing to do with the modern sense of the symmetrical but describes the relationships between the parts and the whole. In that respect it marks the boundaries between normality and the grotesque, between humans and monsters.

The second consideration in establishing character is *rhythm*, the Greek *rhythmos* (ρυθμός). Rhythm, deriving from the verb *rheo*, to flow, suggests a kind of sequential movement dictated by the displacement of matter in space and time. In that sense rhythm establishes character by relating the syncopated elements of a building to its programme (commodity) and construction (firmness).

ABOVE: Stoa of Attalos with the Temple of Theseus in the background, Athens, c 159-138 BC, reconstructed by J Travlos, 1953-56; OPPOSITE TOP LEFT: Pythius, Temple of Athena Polias, Priene, c 340-156 BC; OPPOSITE TOP RIGHT: Curetes street, Ephesus; OPPOSITE BOTTOM: F Boulanger and T Hansen, Zappeion, internal peristyle, Athens, c 1874

In its Greek sense, rhythm gives direction and structured unity to the elements of a building which otherwise would seem random and incoherent. It provides a sense of the whole even though we can only make sense of rhythm by following the individual formal events which it attempts to relate. Rhythm 'forges a synthesis of the heterogeneous'. It is tempting to equate the classical *rhythmos* with our modern notion of composition. But we should be cautious since rhythm as rupture and articulation at the same time, precedes and underlies all figuration and verisimilitude. The Greeks emphasised the regulated aspect of rhythm and its kinetic ordering, which is informed both by dance and music in much the same way as Walter Benjamin discussed it in his *Trauerspiel*, as the 'choric diction' of tragedy.

The third consideration is that of *akribeia* (ἀκρίβεια), which derives from *akron*, peak or point, and suggests sharpness and exactitude. In the practice of the workshops, *akribeia* had the meaning of exacting skill and proficiency in workmanship. Strictly speaking, it meant precision of execution and in the context of classical naturalism it referred also to the faithful representation of nature. By the first century AD, Greek rhetoricians like Demetrius were using the term *akribeia* to describe the specific traits of workmanship embodied in a work. In this sense of workmanship and detailing, *akribeia* becomes an important consideration in establishing character, since it mediates between the intended idea of a work and its material execution.

*   *   *

Let me now turn to a consideration of ornament and the way by which it can be said to ascribe character to a building. How is it that from a manifold stream of impressions certain forms are selected and endowed with a particular decorative significance? Is ornament related to the making of an artefact or is it extrinsic to its structure? Here we must understand that ornament is tied to representation in much the same way as language is tied to use. As language intermeshes with its use in the everyday life from which it obtains its sense, so does ornament participate in the social practices which give it meaning in the first place.

There is, therefore, something to be said for the view that tattooing, hairdressing, ornamental scars and other modes of self-decoration are conferred upon men and women of primitive tribes as outward signs of rank and merit. Ethnologists tell us that the chief aim of tribal self-decoration is *not* to make the man or woman more beautiful or charming but only to show their skill, valour, wealth and rank or as protection against illness, bewitching or the evil eye. The simplest ornaments have been trophies of war and chase, while the most extreme example of commemorative self-decoration has no doubt been a native of Tahiti, named Tepane, who tattooed on his arm a pictorial description of the removal of the great stone idols from his native land now in the British Museum. It is in this sense that we can say that ornament is always determined by its relationship to what it decorates and by what carries it.

It is necessary to recover this ancient insight. Kant, who endorsed this

ABOVE TOP: Capital from the internal peristyle of Zappeion in Athens; ABOVE BOTTOM: Capital from a porch of a house in London: OPPOSITE: Cossutius, Temple of Zeus Olympius, Athens, 174 BC-132 AD

opinion, admits in his famous judgement on tattooing that ornament is ornament 'only when it suits the wearer'. In other words, ornament is not primarily an independent object which is then applied to something else, but rather it is part of the overall presentation of the wearer or of the thing that carries it. This is made clear when we think of everyday expressions such as: 'that dress or that hat suits you'. Fashion, at its most elementary level, is 'ornament that suits the wearer'.

In buildings, ornament can be discussed in terms either of profile or motif. If we turn for a moment to the experience of profile, we see that its origins are twofold: on one hand construction, on the other nature itself. Profile, from the Latin *filare*, to spin, was originally a technical term referring to the specific activity of the weaver and the potter, and soon acquired the sense of a representation in outline. The early origins of profile, therefore, are to be sought in the methods of construction itself.

Construction and fabrication, as we know, imply a deliberate transformation of raw material involving human labour guided by a *techne*. When completed, the final artefact speaks unwittingly of the *techne* that produced it. These marks of its making often assume in the human imagination the status of a picture or an image. Consider for example, different ways of connecting two pieces: each evokes its own image and the physiognomy of the joint is different depending on whether the pieces are stitched, nailed, bolted, clipped, wrapped, tied, etc. In earliest times such images seem to have attained an almost mythic significance. Ethnologists have argued convincingly that the same mythic animation which was bestowed upon the words of human speech was originally accorded to images and to every kind of decorative or artistic representation.

Consider, for example, the case of the *scotia*. Whether it marks the brick, stone, or timber joint, the *scotia* speaks of bringing together two building elements while keeping them apart as discrete units. The *torus* on the other hand speaks of tightening, securing and tying as if by a rope. The *hypotrachelion* or *collar* at the top of the shaft of a column, expresses exactly such an experience. Or consider the craft of stitching and the various decorative forms it has occasioned. These and similar profiles, which may appear to the casual observer as products of spontaneous artistic activity, reveal themselves as commemorative images of construction and fabrication.

In addition to construction, nature itself has often been the source of origin of many profiles. A good example is the Egyptian *cavetto*, which commemorates the lotus or the bending leaves at the topmost termination of the tree. The upright *cavetto*, therefore, cannot be used at the base of the column since its expressive physiognomy derives from the bending leaf. Instead, at the base we find the *torus*, the *scotia* and the inverted *cavetto*. Here the *torus* does not express the experience of tying or binding; rather it expresses the deformation due to vertical pressure, as when we step on an inflated bag. When used at the base, therefore, the profile of the *torus* expresses the load that the base of the column carries and distributes to the stylobate. Or consider the sinuous line of a *cymation* supporting a cornice: its profile, as confirmed by its name, derives from the outline of a small

ABOVE TOP & BOTTOM: Paeonius of Ephesus and Daphnis of Miletus, Temple of Apollo at Didyma, column bases of the pronaos, c 313 BC-41 AD; OPPOSITE TOP LEFT & RIGHT: Temple of Isis, capitals from court colonnades, Island of Philae, c 283-47 BC; OPPOSITE BOTTOM: Hiera Stoa, Priene, c 158-130 BC

ABOVE TOP: Temple of Amon-Ra, pillars in Hall of Tuthmosis III, c 1450 BC; ABOVE MIDDLE: Pilaster from a subterranean room in the Temple of Jerusalem, after Charles Chipiez, Le Temple de Jerusalem, *1889; ABOVE BOTTOM: The nautilus shell as an example of helix found in nature; OPPOSITE TOP & BOTTOM: Hellenistic details of volutes from the Temples of Dionysus at Pergamum and Apollo at Didyma, c 2nd century BC*

wave and reminds one of the momentary dancing of raindrops as they are gently blown by the breeze.

The generating geometry of classical profiles is indeed astonishingly simple. Based on the ellipse or the circle, the basic profiles are the *cavetto* and *ovolo*, the *scotia* and *torus*, the *cyma recta* and *cyma reversa*, while the right angle gives the *taenia*. The combinations and variations of these primary profiles, however, are infinite. By means of superimposition, inclination of their generating axes and selection of partial segments, an infinite number of profiles can be produced while their character can be expressively varied.

The same varied expression of character also derives from the enrichment of profiles. The anthemion models the surface of the *cyma recta*; the egg and dart that of the *ovolo*, the bead and reel of the *astragal* while the fret enriches the flat *taenia*. Finally, to the expressive character of profile one must add the humanising effect of the classical Greek refinements, as for example the entasis of the column and the stylobate, the upward curvature of the entablature below the pediment, or the perspectival adjustment of parabolic mouldings. Whether these were intended as optical corrections or tokens of expressive freedom is a debate which cannot be settled here. It remains true, however, that classical Greek buildings owe their special character of presence to such refinements.

Turning now to classical ornamental motifs, we find that they never derive from within architecture; their origins cannot be traced back to building techniques. Many are realistic or stylised motifs drawn from nature. Others are symbolic or allegorical motifs relating to the sphere of social life and mythology. Nature is shown, for example, in the acanthus leaf, while the classical volute imitates the helix found in the snail or the seashell. Egyptian architecture is dominated by phytomorphic forms and presents renderings of the lotus and papyrus in bud form or full-blossom, complex, multifolded or simple. Similar phytomorphic and zoomorphic forms can be found in all traditional architecture as with the Indian holy animals or the Gothic griffins.

From social mythology derive ornamental motifs like the egg and dart symbolising life and death or the rope and wreath which in antiquity was a symbol of fertility. The subjects of mythological motifs vary extensively and reflect social relationships or attitudes people have taken towards nature and their gods. These motifs pertain to a reality that is experienced as ritual and their true home is in legendary accounts. Ritual processions, mythological figures of gods, symbolic attributes and images, all contribute to the iconographic heritage of ornamental motifs. But perhaps the most significant allegorical contribution of classical architecture has been its constant allusion to the human body. The base, the shaft, the capital, the hypotrachelion, the annulets, all underline the similarity of columns to human bodies. This correspondence is not merely a manner of speaking; the caryatids, the telamones or the titans, all attest to such an anthropomorphic vision.

This brings me to the social and, therefore historical (as opposed to ontological) nature of ornamental motifs. If profiles have their origin in

construction and motifs in custom, it should not be unreasonable to expect that motifs have a shorter life-span. Once old rites, customs and practices have weakened, their mythical experience becomes a mere element of form. While we should note the historical relevance of ornament we must, nonetheless, realise that the ornamental tendency is never absent from architecture whether it is Greek, Egyptian, Byzantine, Gothic, Renaissance, Indian, Chinese, Islamic or otherwise. Together with tectonics, ornament forms the basis out of which any building tradition can hope to grow into architecture.

These examples have shown us how construction, nature and social beliefs are interwoven with ornament. Of its own, ornament is trite; but it finds its purpose in its relation to that which it decorates. This is not to say that classical ornament interprets or explains construction or natural phenomena and social customs. Ornament simply portrays and commemorates. It is precisely this relinquishement of explanations that engages our trust. The stylisation of ornament gives luminosity and firm definition to the otherwise fading impressions of experience.

At the same time classical ornament is never determined by an individual artist. This is perhaps the case with all ornament. Ornamental profiles or motifs cannot be invented as signs or mere tokens. Ornament speaks always of a mythic animation which is bestowed upon construction and upon natural phenomena and social customs. Ornament, like language, is originally bound up entirely with myth. It is only much later that it achieves its purely representational, purely 'aesthetic' role, only as the magic circle with which mythical consciousness surrounds it is broken.

LEFT: Lukas von Hildebrandt, Upper Belvedere, detail of tehamones in the entry hall, Vienna, c 1693-1724; OPPOSITE: D Porphyrios, house in Kensington, view of hall from landing, London, 1987

CHAPTER V

COMMON SENSE

'The new is that which distances itself by constantly focusing on the familiar.'
Wilhelm von Humboldt

'It is not the activity of the present moment but wise reflexions from the past that help us to safeguard the future.'
Marcel Proust, Remembrance of Things Past

There is a growing sense that we should take stock of the achievements of twentieth-century architecture and urbanism. Most contemporary debates are still structured within the intellectual framework set up by the Modernists of the twenties and thirties. There is still an underlying belief that, in the final analysis, the only viable alternatives open to us are either some form of experimentalism or that we are led ineluctably to regressive historicism. The recent experience of Post-Modernism has proven – if anything – that contemporary architectural culture is not capable of 'making friends' with history. History is still seen through the spectacles of Modernist architecture: not as moral education but merely as the repository of stylistic frivolity. In spite of recent attempts to exorcise history by wearing its clothes, architects and theoreticians alike still draw conclusions similar to those drawn in the twenties and thirties: namely that history nurtures no moral paradigms; it simply points to a value-free relativism. Whether it concerns the plan for a city, the design of a building or the beauty of an architectural detail, we are told that all judgement is relative to a specific form of society and life.

This scepticism about guiding principles seems to be characteristic of our intellectual life. We are told that it is an illusion to think that there are enduring standards of common sense to which we can appeal in order to understand and judge the competing claims that are continuously made by architects and critics. We are told that, in our search for principles, we are limited to our historical context and by the 'Spirit of the Age'. In fact, we are told that the 'Spirit of our Age' is not only a sacred boundary we cannot trespass but that in this concept alone shines the beam of truth, credibility and reason.

These and similar attitudes towards the history of architecture and urbanism are, admittedly, as much in vogue today as they were fifty or sixty years ago. This conception of history constantly flirts with the suggestion that what we take to be true, right or beautiful is invariably arbitrary. It

OPPOSITE: View of Town Hall, Patmos, mid-19th century

follows, therefore, that since there can be no enduring values, anything goes. Anything goes as long as it is marked by an internal, self-regulating (and thus self-legitimating) method. Here lies the source of our demand that if an architectural project is to be judged fairly, it should be judged on the basis of its proclaimed aims, standards and values. Architecture and urbanism are thus made adjuncts to the demands of opportunism, or at best to the conceits of agnosticism.

It is true that today we tend to reject spontaneously any idea of a canon that normalises artistic and architectural activity. And yet it is also true that a select repertory of buildings from the past continues to be a part of even the most modest architectural education. In fact, considerable financial resources and a large section of the media are still reserved for the nurturing of the 'classics'. How can such an acceptance of tradition be reconciled with its simultaneous rejection?

Since this subject is so enormous I ask you to consider one or two points. Take, for example, the *Querelle* which questioned for the first time since the end of the Middle Ages the normative value granted to the art and literature of the ancients. Once artists and architects stopped adhering to standards of taste, exemplary works disappeared and were substituted by individualistic and singular ones. Without a canon of exemplars and no frame of reference, artistic judgement also lost its authority and had to be justified solely by the criterion of novelty and individualism.

We see this very clearly in our schools, in the statements of professional competition juries, in the writings of critics and in the buildings erected around us everyday. A very telling paradox, I should add, characterises recent Modernist architectural education: the very Modernists who preach liberation from norms produce their own textbooks and canons. They forego the 'banal' pleasure of continuity for a more acute, if more dismaying, pleasure that arises from the experience of loss and transgression. And yet they institute their own canons and endow them with an aura of radiance such as had not graced even the most canonical artists of antiquity. This is of course double play: De(con)struction's desire to have it both ways, to be in the community, but not of it. These are the 'stuntmen' of Modernist education today. But though stunters are, admittedly, very useful in the performance and entertainment industry, in Modernist art and architecture I believe them to be the expression of an embarrassment for which quasi-intellectual arguments must be found.

It may be that to be conscious of this state of affairs means to recognise the critical potential that classical architecture and traditional urbanism possess today. I mention this because seventy years ago classical humanism was ousted from its central position in Western art and architecture – though not among ordinary people. Since then there has been a great deal made of nonsense, novelty and invention in art. But today we have come full circle and have started to value tradition once again; not for its prescriptive rules but for its perpetual modernity.

The question that the classical project raises today is how to look at architecture and urbanism as a discipline that invites new appraisals of the

ABOVE: GB del Tasso, Mercato Nuovo, Florence, c 1547; OPPOSITE TOP & BOTTOM: The urban tradition of building blocks, streets and squares: examples from Venice and Seville

relation between permanence and change. Technology may serve here as an example. To be sure we may refuse to accept the claim made by traditionalists that modern building technology is virtually non-existent, but we may also have reason to be sceptical of the Modernist claim that technology is an instrument for human progress. Classicism's own question remains valid: how are we to assess the technological mobilisation of humanity and the earth at the beginning of the twenty-first century?

The problem as stated is not just an intellectual one, nor is it confined to parochial or dated disputes about this dialogue between permanence and change. At issue are our everyday ethical and political experiences. Are we to believe that there are moral objectives of the true, the good and the beautiful and social and political objectives of the just, or are we to relegate the definition of such norms to chance or individual fancy?

Ever since Plato, many have argued that relativism is self-contradictory and paradoxical since the relativist claims that although his position is true, it may also be false, given that truth is relative. In his turn, the relativist accuses the rationalist of mistaking what is at best historically or culturally stable for the eternal and permanent. When the rationalist claims that it is necessary to establish evaluative criteria for the design of architecture and the city, the relativist argues that there is something fraudulent about such claims and that, since life is complex and multi-faceted, anyone striving for clarity of understanding must be by definition a *terrible simplificateur*. But then again the rationalist argues that the fashionable varieties of relativism and the enthusiasm for an endless playfulness of interpretation that knows no rules and no limits have always led to cynicism and ultimately to a growing sense of trivialisation.

This debate has grown in prominence since the mid nineteen-sixties. At the same time, indiscriminate toleration, posing as the guarantor of democratic freedom, has thrown our cities into disarray, undermining our everyday lives. By contrast, a few have sought to reappraise the 'march of progress' hailed by Modernist architecture and urbanism. They have criticised the Modernist industrial city for its urban sprawl, its land-use zoning, its megastructural scale, its senseless technological gadgetry, its rapid turnover and speedy obsolescence, its ephemeral constructional systems, its rampant loss of historical memory and the jaded or affected taste of its chic avant-garde.

The point, I should add, is one that Classicism makes and has made in the past in a more general way. In a culture where 'everybody is (meant to be) original', the classical is that which questions the very meaning of originality itself. In fact, the classical goes as far as admitting and even embracing the voice of others. This gives the classical project at once a background and a richness of diversity which the practitioner of 'novelty' cannot hope to achieve. The classical, then, demonstrates that despite the vagaries of historical time, there can be, and – indeed there do exist – continuities and common-sense principles.

But the idea of suggesting common-sense principles at all has been – at least recently – a repudiated conception. In many ways it has also been

ABOVE: Mosque of Khalif al-Hakim, Cairo, Fatimid period, c 990-1013; OPPOSITE: Madrasa of Sultan Barquq, Cairo, Mamluk period, c 1384-86

73

repellent. Why? Because it offers no rewards to the experimentalist and, in the name of reason, it appears to consort with the grossest of our superstitions: metaphysics. Worst of all, it attacks liberal morality at its most vulnerable spot: its self-esteem as *the* age of pluralist toleration.

In the background of all these issues the question remains as to how credible and how universal common-sense principles can hope to be today. Three related questions are at present at the very centre of much discussion about the classical. First, why claim, in the first place, that there exist (or ought to exist) common-sense principles of architecture and urbanism? Second, where are we to look for, and how are we to obtain, such principles? Third, how can we apply them without lapsing into vulgar or sophisticated forms of unwarranted authoritarianism?

Historically the source for the conviction that common-sense principles do exist has of course been, Vitruvius, Filarete or Alberti. But whereas for Classical Antiquity and the Renaissance this foundation of certainty was God's divinity, for the post-Enlightenment world of modernity human reason was to take the place of God. Descartes' *Meditations* stands as the great rationalist treatise of modern times and his demand that we should rely upon the authority of reason alone has itself been at the very centre of modern life. In his *Critique of Pure Reason*, Kant also describes 'the domain (of pure reason) as an island, enclosed by nature itself within unalterable limits. It is the land of truth – enchanting name! – surrounded by a wide and stormy ocean, the native home of illusion . . .'

Reading the classical project as a search for a foundation point, we are at the same time aware that the ghost hovering in the background is the Kantian dread of madness, of the 'wide and stormy ocean, the native home of illusion', of the chaos where nothing is familiar. *Either* there exists a common sense that informs architecture and the city, *or* we are left with the wayward alternatives of opportunism and agnosticism. Such is the ultimate motivation for the search for principles. It stems neither from religious zeal nor from avarice. It is neither bigotry nor power-hunting. The urge to search for certainty is a fundamental attribute of human character.

Where are we to look for such principles of common sense? The quest for a paradigm begins as soon as we first confront the desecrated landscape of our cities and the impoverishment of our artistic imagination. The misery of the industrial city that we witness every day brings to mind the prescient statement by Lewis Mumford on the role of twentieth-century *anti*-art: 'Anti-art . . . acclimatises modern man to the habitat that megatechnics is bringing into existence; an environment degraded by garbage dumps, auto cemeteries, slag heaps, nuclear piles, superhighways and megastructural conglomerates – all destined to be architecturally homogenised in a planetary Megalopolis.' In a similar indictment, the classical project today accuses the twentieth-century industrial state of usurping humanity by creating – in Seidelberg's terms – the 'Post-Historic Man': the ironic end product of evolution, achieved through the hypertrophy of either intelligence or mechanical power; a hypertrophy that would eventually return man to 'a state of docile somnolence'.

ABOVE: Street in Corfu, mid-19th century; OPPOSITE TOP: Martino Lombardo, Scuola di S Marco, Venice, c 1485-95; OPPOSITE BOTTOM: Michelangelo, Capitol, Rome, c 1546

Faced with the alienating docility of the industrial world, the city – if it is to live again – must become a *Città Felice*. Surely, the city as a setting for a life both productive, pleasurable and morally sane lies within the authentic tradition of Plato and the Renaissance humanists. What present-day Classicism takes from the ancients is the essential definition of the *Città Felice* as shown in the ideas of *disegno* and *misura*.

Let me be more explicit. The architect ought to enshrine the ideal in a *disegno* for reality to approximate. The *disegno* never exists as an empirical reality. It is a paradigm, an exemplar that guides and which, insofar as it is not a model to be copied, never runs the risk of trivialisation through cloning. The *disegno* insofar as it is an exemplar, does not curtail interpretive freedom nor does it shy away from contingent reality. If anything, the *disegno* becomes a real city-plan only when it is interpreted under the stringent pressures of everyday contingent life. In this sense, design does not refer merely to the formal, functional, or financial resolution of a given problem. It rather refers to a wider guiding vision that articulates the goals and aspirations of the community at large. In fact, the growing awareness of the necessity for a balanced ecosystem makes the classical idea of *disegno* even more prescient and timely today.

At the same time, the *Città Felice* depends also on *misura*. Measure, proportion, size (whether understood as dimensioning a city's urban space or as the finitude of the city's extent) are, in the end, the guarantors of the ultimate success of a *disegno*. A city without proper measure is like Aristotle's ill-dimensioned ship which will never sail. And yet, the paradigm of the *Città Felice* is not to be sought in the walled cities of antiquity but in the millenial history of the traditional city: for it alone shines as the embodiment of urban wisdom. Its *disegno* unfolds along the well-trodden and familiar forms of the urban block, the street, the piazza and the monument. And its *misura* has long since become to us second nature.

Such re-evaluation of the traditional city does not grow out of antiquarianism. Any serious comparative investigation of the historical beginnings and growth of traditional cities reveals principles that are concealed in the diversity of their forms. This is no mystical or idealistic position that views the multiplicity of forms as mere corruptions of some abstract, *a priori* truth. Instead, the numerous traditional cities, in their historical specificity and detail, bear witness to a common and humanly satisfying *disegno* and *misura*.

To proclaim, and indeed to feel, a principal allegiance to the Traditional City does not necessarily involve a patronising attitude towards some European *Heimatstil*. There have been many European architects and planners who have chosen the perilous path of the megalopolis and the Las Vegas Strip; perhaps as a means to shed the stigmata that compromised their opportunities; perhaps because they thought this way they would be seen as belonging truly to 'their Age'. But good cities are not made by always going along with what the traffic engineers, the planning bureaucracy or the building industry propose, simply because of fears of being left out. Instead good city plans are both productive and pleasurable only when they manage to articulate the contingencies of everyday life with the aspirations of the

ABOVE: Bernardo Rosellino, Central Piazza at Pienza, c 1458-62; OPPOSITE TOP: Family graves of Schliemann (Architect E Ziller), Theologos and Koupas, 1st Cemetery of Athens, c 1890; OPPOSITE BOTTOM: Kaisariani Monastery, ancillary buildings, late 11th century

community at large.

Still, it takes two to make the paradigm of the Traditional City credible. Many in the audience, especially those bred in imminent cynicism, applaud the classicists for their zeal but are inclined to find their paradigm unconvincing. Why? The reasons have been as varied as the sophist's tricks. Some find the paradigm of the Traditional City too sentimental for their proven sense of realism; others find it quasi-socialist and therefore prone to youthful idealism and error; many call it a utopia, for they themselves have given up hope; yet others accuse such a global project of siding dangerously with neo-Fascism.

The main reservation of all critics, however, has been that the adoption of the Traditional City as an urban paradigm is a gross setback to the idea of progress. Critics maintain that traditional forms of urbanisation have in the past proven dangerous setbacks to the economic, political and cultural progress of civilisation. Tradition, critics repeat, considers a changeless state of order as the greatest good and, as a result, it fosters an authoritarianism that invariably stifles progress.

I shall return to this subject of tradition in my next chapter. Here one must only note that classicists of course know that their adversaries are calling them doctrinaire and authoritarian and they regret the metaphors used to discredit them. To the best of their knowledge, however, they are neither powerful *podestàs* nor infallible Popes. If they insist on their findings it is simply because the Traditional City has proven to be a working and adaptable model. What is the source that inspires such self-assurance? On a pragmatic level there is the idea that the well-trodden and known forms of the Traditional City have proven successful from the time of the ancients down to the present day. Though the world has changed enormously in the last thousand years or so, the urban structure of the Traditional City has endured. There seems to exist no reason, therefore, for doubting the paradigm's validity, for there have been no failures. If all available information leads one to believe that the goal of the twentieth-century city – namely the well-being of its citizens – need not be different from that of previous civilisations, then it is good common sense to use a time-tested body of knowledge to cope with present-day exigencies.

But Classicism does not simply offer a pragmatic argument in support of its paradigm. The legitimisation of tradition is to be grounded not merely on efficacy. It must stand the scrutiny of argumentation, the criterion for which is neither pragmatism nor historicism nor logical formalism. The ultimate criterion is the public well-being of the city's inhabitants.

Let me now suggest that the apparent banality of the expression 'public well-being' shows the inadequacy of contemporary language when confronted with the essential nature of the city. And let me further suggest that the issues that come into prominence in connection with the paradigm of the Traditional City open up an ethical dimension in the debate about the essential nature of the city itself. To grasp the ethical dimension of the expression 'public well-being' we should for a moment examine two constitutive ideas of classical thought: those of tradition and reconstruction.

ABOVE: Giacomo da Vignola and Bartolomeo Ammanati, Villa Giulia, view of portico, c 1551-55; OPPOSITE TOP: A Palladio, Villa Badoer, Fratta Polesine, (Rovigo), c 1557; OPPOSITE BOTTOM: Giovanni and Bartolomeo Buon, Doge's Palace, view of the court, Venice, c 1309-1424

Unlike the currently marketed conception of tradition as the 'peddling of antiques', the classical project does not aim at upholstering a spurious restoration. Instead, its aim has been to ferret out in existing society those traditional elements that could foster the new. The story of cities has been the story of endless innovation. But the new has never been a mere novelty. The new has always been the result of a process of transmission of knowledge and merit. The various phases of history are additive and the storing of new experience has been the law of mankind. The exclusive characteristic of civilised man has been his ability to record and retrieve from memory. In that sense, Classicism and the Traditional City are less absorbed in the dialectic between an imagined future and a nostalgic past (as many critics have claimed) than in the search for realistic projects. The ultimate criterion in the design of cities ought to be the public well-being of their inhabitants. *Le bien public* is the supreme law that ought to govern every urban project. We must remember that the notion of public well-being does not refer to some faceless universalism. On the contrary, individuals as well as local communities can and must preserve their particular character as complete and fully grown entities. By definition, however, good social institutions – and by extension good city plans – are those that are best able to instil in man a social existence and 'to translate the *moi* into a *moi-commun*', a collective ethical self (Jean-Jacques Rousseau, *Emile*). The central issue here is not the nature of ethical understanding but rather the wider question of the extent to which the State, social institutions and major patrons should be committed to conceptions of public good, that is, to what is worthwhile in human life. It is this yearning for a collective ethical self that Classicism makes the cornerstone of its urban theory.

Such is the ethical content of the classical paradigm: over the centuries the Traditional City has contributed to mollifying the antagonism between the *moi* (individual) and the *moi commun* (community) by providing a careful balance of public and private spaces and buildings as the physical frame-work for the life of its citizens. And inversely, here lies the root of the failure of the Modernist industrial city: over the last century it has aggravated the antagonism between the *moi* and the *moi-commun* either by marketing the rapacity of the entrepreneur in the name of realism or by mistaking the collective body with a mere numerical majority. The Modernist city has tragically failed; firstly by strengthening the savage instinct of entrepreneurial interests and secondly by confounding democracy with the sloppiest of all delusions: spontaneous populist egalitarianism.

Above all, and despite the tensions that might exist in contemporary debates, the classical project illuminates the fragile character of action as *reconstruction*. It is not a sentimental utopia that we confront here but a coherent and powerful 'What is to be done?' that has a clear commitment and direction. When one insists that the making of the city requires the shared acceptance of civic priorities one assumes, at least in an incipient form, that even today practical reason (reason applied in conduct) has not foresaken us totally. Despite the fact that *techne* (craft as practical reason) has degenerated into *technique* (labour as technical reason) there are still

ABOVE: Interior of Byzantine church at Mystras; OPPOSITE: Cosmosoteira Church, Chios, c 1060

solidarities of civic consciousness which could revitalise practical reason. A city is not something that can be engineered by any form of technique and by any chosen administration. That would be similar to claiming that any street garbage (nowadays called *objet trouvé*) hanging on the walls of a museum is art. Or, to return to Plato, it would be similar to giving the name 'true musicians' to any of those 'who would invent their own instruments and play on them any disharmonious tune . . .' The idea that we can engineer cities by simply applying any technical know-how has been the typically Modernist response to urbanism and has proven disastrous. The failures of positivist planning have been mainly due to the decision of industrial society to restrict itself to the sole horizon of technique at the expense of common-sense practical reason. The chief task of urbanism today, however, is to challenge the peculiar falsehood of Modernist industrial consciousness and to defend practical reason against the domination of universal technique.

The idea of reconstruction – as opposed to mere urban renewal – points, therefore, to a practical-ethical project. For there exists a different relationship between means and ends in reconstruction than in urban renewal. The aim of reconstruction, unlike that of urban renewal, is the public well-being and not a particular end-product. Moreover, while urban renewal is not concerned with the means that allow it to arrive at an end, this is precisely what is required in reconstruction. The meaning and task of reconstruction today is to elicit in us the will that can become a counterforce against the contemporary degeneration of practical reason and common sense.

*   *   *

Throughout my discussion I have sought to elicit the central themes of tradition and reconstruction. I have stressed the practical and politico-ethical consequences of these themes – for as one explores their implications, they draw one towards the goal of action and practical reason (reason applied in conduct). If we take classical thought seriously and press its own claims, they lead us beyond the sentimentalities of historicism. It is in the very nature of man to be confronted with conflicts which require of him that he exercises his ethical judgement. Surely, there is never full certainty of good judgement or of a happy ending. But only in meeting these challenges can we 'tame the freedom of the will without stifling it'.

Such a perspective avoids the cultural relativism and professional neutrality of today's sceptics. It also rescues us from the self-indulgent antiquarianism of the 'Heritage' industry. We must remember that the classical is rooted in a perception of history as a continual renaissance: a movement that establishes continuities by means of constant renovation rather than through dogmatic canons. For it is true that the more a work of architecture or a city plan is opened to new interpretations, the more its classical status is reinforced. It is in that sense that we can say that the future depends neither on abstract concepts of development and progress, nor on the random play of chance. It depends on our skill in using that capacity for common-sense reason and judgement which has already brought us so far.

ABOVE: KF Schinkel, Schloss Glienicke, Berlin, 1824-1827; OPPOSITE: D Porphyrios, Belvedere Farm, central hall and tower, Ascot, 1990

literature of classical antiquity. I say 'useful convention' because this view grossly underestimates the contribution of other periods to the problem of break-versus-continuity with the ancients. Consider, for example, the practices of *inventio* in Roman oratory, of the *translatio studii* in Medieval scholasticism, of the Renaissance *renovatio* of antiquity, or of the sixteenth century Ciceronian Quarrel. They all bear precisely on the question of deciding whether absolute models can be selected from antiquity and to what extent tradition can be a source of inspiration or a futile constraint. But in spite of these qualifications, it remains true that the Enlightenment differed from all these attitudes in one characteristic way: it decided everything before the judgement of reason. The authority of the ancients, therefore, was seen as a source of prejudice. And though the Enlightenment's criticism was directed primarily against the religious tradition of the Bible, there was the general feeling that all tradition was tainted with covert guile.

At first sight this view of authority as the seat of prejudice seems obvious. The etymological foundation of the idea of prejudice, however, shows us a different experience. Judging (*krinein*, κρίνειν) for the Greeks was a matter of parting, dividing out and selecting. But in order to sift the material under examination we must at least have a preliminary view. We find such an idea of pre-judgement (*prokrisis*, πρόκρισις) in Plato and the use of the term carries no sense of perjury or false judgement. This pre-judgement is a sort of preliminary understanding that marks the point of departure for all thought and action. In this sense, prejudice as pre-judgement is our everyday relationship to the world as a necessary condition of intelligibility and grounding. From the point of view both of the individual and the collective community, prejudice describes our social competence: it provides a socially constructed know-how with which to face the world, and grounds this knowledge on actions already symbolically mediated by common sense.

We should not underestimate the social importance of this initial grounding in the world 'as found and as handed down to us'. A prejudice is a sort of pre-judgement that gives us a background. Without such a background we cannot recognise ourselves nor can we set out questioning ourselves. This is seen very clearly in education when a teacher needs to balance the different 'backgrounds' of his students or when the student projects his own reading (prejudice) and thereby transforms the teacher's intended statement. All art and interpretation plays upon this oscillation between prejudice and understanding.

This is where we find ourselves today and this is why I have examined the discrediting by the Enlightenment of all authority as prejudice. But let me go over this argument once again. The Enlightenment draws a distinction between faith in authority and faith in one's own reason. I suppose this distinction is legitimate; when authority tramples over reason then its claim is a perjury. But this does not mean that authority cannot also be a source of reason. And yet in the context of Enlightenment thought the concept of authority was vilified and blackened. Authority was given the meaning of blind obedience to power and force. Authority was made synonymous with

ABOVE TOP: A Palladio, Villa Pojana, Pojana Maggiore, (Vicenza), c 1549; ABOVE BOTTOM: D Porphyrios, House in Kensington, view of conservatory, London, 1987; OPPOSITE TOP: Temple of Hadrian, Ephesus, c 117-138 AD; OPPOSITE BOTTOM: Bartolomeo Ammanati, Villa Giulia, view of the Nymphaeum loggia, Rome, 1551-55

authoritarianism. And all authoritative sources became authoritarian.

This is not, of course, the meaning of authority. Those who have authority base it ultimately not on the surrender of reason but on knowledge itself. When we say, 'he is an authority on brain surgery', we mean that he is superior to ourselves and everybody we know of in the knowledge of brain surgery. For this reason his judgement (on matters regarding brain surgery) takes precedence; that is, it has priority over ours. What an authority states, therefore, is *not* irrational or arbitrary but can be seen to be true. Occasionally in life we meet such people whose authority imparts to their speech and presence an 'added weight.' Language has actually recorded this very simple experience. The Greek word for authority (*kyros*, κύρος) derives from the Indo-Germanic *ku* which has the sense of an 'added weight and growth'. The pregnant woman (ἔγκυος) or, similarly, the wave that builds up as it approaches the shore (κῦμα) are two examples of this early physical sense of growth. Similarly, the Latin *auctor*, the author who brings about the existence of an object derives from *aucto* (*augeo*) which initially had the sense of increase, enlargement or augmentation. We can see, therefore, how the early sense of authority had to do with physical growth and weight.

As language became metaphorical, this early sense was *not* lost: still today, an authoritative statement is one which appears to have 'added weight'. Authority, in other words, cannot be bestowed but must be acquired on account of wisdom if someone is to lay claim to it. It is this passage into the social that gives meaning, say, to the authority of the teacher or the leader. Their authority has nothing to do with obedience and command but rather with reason and knowledge.

But is there another kind of authority that is different from those of the leader, the learned man or the teacher? At first sight it seems that the authority of tradition is indeed different in as much as it determines our everyday attitudes and institutions. And whereas all other authority answers to reason, the authority of tradition appears to be self-validating, at once imperious and natural.

I do not think, however, that such a 'natural' tradition exists or has ever existed. Even the most long-lived traditions in religion, in art or in science did not endure by nature because of habitual laziness or inertia. The authority of tradition does not rest on a *carte-blanche* code of trust. Instead, tradition has to be embraced and cultivated. The very idea of education itself hinges on this. For even though the teacher loses his authority when the pupil matures and forms his own insights, this passage into maturity does *not* mean that a person has repudiated tradition. On the contrary, he has made tradition his own. It is precisely in this passage into maturity that the 'wonder' of education lies. Education exists only when tradition is freely taken over.

What does it mean, however, 'to take over tradition freely'? It is true that in our attitude to the past we always stand within tradition. What I mean here is that we do *not* think of tradition as something foreign to ourselves, imposed as a means of censorship and control. Consider for a moment one's own language and the way it is handed down to us. It is not forced upon us

ABOVE: F Brunelleschi, Pazzi Chapel, Santa Croce, Florence, c 1430; OPPOSITE: A Palladio, Palazzo Iseppo-Porto, Vicenza, c 1552

against our will nor is it left over by accident or chance. Linguistic tradition is always given to us in the sense that we grow in it whether in the re-enactment forms of play, custom, speaking or writing. What tradition hands down to us is a sort of knowledge that allows us to relate to the world by means of familiarity and recognition. In this sense tradition is always part of us for in it we recognise ourselves. Consider, for example, the case of learning a new language. In the beginning, French or Finnish is always something alien and outside ourselves; we stumble over it and it is an impediment to thinking. However, once we master a foreign language, we can hardly see it as an acquired knowledge but rather as a tradition that was always there. This is what I mean when I say that tradition is always part of us. This is the sense in which it could be said that in our everyday life we 'take over tradition freely,' that is, of our own free will.

But what of those artistic traditions towards which we have developed a sense of loss and estrangement? Are such traditions irredeemably cut off from our understanding? Or can they be regained and, if so, what might be the relevance of such a new life?

Opinion here, as we know, is and has been divided. Broadly speaking two positions have been argued. There are those who maintain that if removed from its original context the work of art loses its significance. Being the product of a specific people and of a particular period the work of art can be understood only in terms of the conditions of its origin. Hence the theories according to which art is the reflection of its culture, and, hence, the studious search by historians for a total reconstruction of the past and for the re-establishment of the original context within which the work of art was first produced. According to this view, historical scholarship brings back what is lost and illuminates tradition, in the sense of retrieving the circumstances of the past and restoring the world as it was in its full documentary significance. This version of historical understanding celebrates an enshrined world and invites us to rehearse it liturgically. Tradition is perceived as fixed beyond change and criticism as if it were a sacred original moment which we should all strive to regain by a ritualistic enactment. This attitude is generally known as revivalism. It promises the restitution of past life and, ultimately, it reduces history into cosy and pacifying fetishes.

In contrast, Hegel, in his *Aesthetics*, puts forward another attitude towards tradition. Hegel understood clearly the futility of revivalism when he wrote that the works of the Muses '. . . have become what they are for us now – beautiful fruit already picked from the tree, fruit which a friendly Fate has offered us . . .' All art belongs to the past: it remains 'fruit picked from the tree'. To re-create the historical context surrounding the production of a work of art does *not* give us a living relationship with art for '. . . the statues are now only stones from which the living soul has flown.' The miraculous dwelling of the spirit in the very forms of classical art is no longer possible in our romantic (modern) world. Scholarship cannot bring back the past; at best it can offer only a historical understanding. This understanding which art-history affords us, argues Hegel, stems only from an external activity.

ABOVE: Sacred lake next to Temple of Hathor, Dendera, c 110 BC-68 AD; OPPOSITE TOP: Bernardo Rossellino, Central Piazza at Pienza, c 1458-62; OPPOSITE BOTTOM LEFT: Courtyard of a house in Cairo, Mamluk period; OPPOSITE BOTTOM RIGHT: Residential square in Corfu, c mid-19th century

The tradition which the art-historian studies is always an external object of research. It is as if on one side there is tradition; and on the other it is us. We look at tradition from outside and we engage in historical research so that we may 'educate' ourselves about the past.

Hence the extreme historicism and relativism of Hegel. Tradition becomes a self-referential system and soon history becomes historiography. We see this happening every day in most art and architectural history courses taught in our schools. And while art-history students can at least graduate once they show proficiency in historiography, we architects are left totally bewildered. The Hegelian reduction of all history to historiography has made it impossible to integrate studio instruction with history courses in a significant manner. The student is presented with history as an objectifying process with no criteria of evaluation. He observes history, so to speak, from outside. The relevance of the historical models he studies is always a matter of arbitrary conjecture or simply of individual taste. It is understandable, therefore, why some repudiate tradition altogether and concentrate on their 'so called' creative intuition, while the rest flirt with the history of civilisation indiscriminately as if it were a mere succession of charming styles.

My view on the subject of tradition is neither with those who preach revivalism nor with the advocates of historical relativism. To understand what tradition is (and specifically, in the context of these series of talks, what the tradition of classical architecture is) we have to ask the question of the relationship of one (classical) building to another. Once we formulate the question this way, two considerations become important: convention and originality.

The study of conventions is based on analogies of form. It is clear that any classical building (and this applies equally to all classic architecture we speak of as enduring) may be studied not only as an imitation of the world and of construction, but as an imitation of other buildings as well. Virgil thought, Pope reminds us, that imitating nature was ultimately the same thing as imitating Homer. Once we think of a classical building in relation to other classical buildings, we can see that a great part of creative design addresses the formation and transformation of conventions. All art and architecture is equally conventionalised, but we do not notice this because such conventions are always meant to appear natural and universal, otherwise their role as the binding 'cement' of society would be undermined. In fact, conventions can best be studied when one travels, for unless we are unaccustomed to the conventions of a country they do *not* stand out. The same is true with the conventions of art and architecture.

Today, however, the conventional element in architecture is elaborately disguised. Consider for example the Modernist slogan 'down with conventions; long live the free spirit of experimentation'. Though such slogans were useful in the formative period of the nineteen-twenties, they became meaningless once Modernist architecture established itself. There have been, of course, a few for whom modernity had meant a permanent state of crisis. According to this view architecture is always *in extremis*. And yet,

ABOVE: House with porch in Seychelles; OPPO-SITE TOP: Otto Wagner, First Villa Wagner, Vienna, 1886-88; OPPOSITE BOTTOM: Jacopo Sansovino, Libreria Sansoviniana, San Marco, Venice c 1537

even the recent deconstructionist mood of transgression relies heavily on the conventional element. In fact, deconstruction does *not* deny the conventional element; it cannot by its own definition as the 'bad conscience' of conventions. It simply suspends the conventional meaning and indulges in playful dadaism. For all its apocalyptic rhetoric, the claim of deconstruction that it is an end to convention can never be made good: for at best it is 'another' set of conventions rather than an end to convention.

There is another factor today that disguises the importance of tradition and the conventional element in architecture: copyright laws. As we all know, the market ethic of the original and the authentic is based on the pretence that every work of art is an invention singular enough to be patented. Ironically, this state of affairs would make it difficult to appraise an architectural tradition which includes, say, Palladio, much of whose architecture is paraphrased from others, or Schinkel, whose buildings sometimes follow their sources almost *verbatim*. The comparison between the Villa Malcontenta and that at Garches comes to mind. And though this particular example might be admirable exactly because it is so far fetched, it is Colin Rowe who made us see that Le Corbusier's building remains in part unintelligible if we do not recognise Palladio in it. Similarly, if we turn to poetry for a moment I am reminded of Milton who asked for nothing better than to borrow the whole of the Bible.

Let me qualify this observation to avoid misunderstanding. Borrowing here does not mean reproducing. The distance between a new work and the model that has inspired it is indeed always the hallmark of creative talent, pointing out the contemporaneity of the work. An artist is said to be original exactly when he takes up the challenge of tradition and makes us see something more than we already know. Originality, and thus the modern itself, consists in this distance between the new and the model as the new emplots itself within tradition. Doubtless, some would argue that the new has no tradition whatsoever. Derrida's *itérabilité* for example, refers exactly to such an aimless 'drift' inherent in all language. Language, cut off from any sense of home-base, is a meandering away from any origins and from all cultural and social meaning. Neither the forms of art nor the words of language, however, are 'orphaned' (as Derrida would have them) but they always acquire a parenthood in the context of the tradition that adopts them. Out of the interplay between 'drift' and repetition each form acquires its unique itinerary. Art is situated exactly at this mid point: art deals neither with origins nor with creation *ex novo* but with the distance traversed between the model and its modern repetition. It is precisely this distance between the model and its imitative repetition that art quite consciously confronts and builds deliberately into the artefact. Art points to a dependence on the models that it conditionally overcomes so that it may formulate its own modernity. 'Imitate so that you may be original', has always been a working principle in art.

At the same time we should realise that the conception of a great architect entrusted with a heritage must become once again as elementary to us as it was to Alberti. And yet, such an attitude would seem to violate the principle

ABOVE: The skyline of Sultan Ahmet Camii, seen from upper gallery of Haghia Sophia, Constantinople, c 1609-16; OPPOSITE TOP: Anthemius of Tralles and Isidorus of Miletus, Haghia Sophia, Constantinople, c 532-37; OPPOSITE BOTTOM: Kapnikarea Church, Athens, c 1060-70

of creation *ex nihilo* that most of us have been taught today.

Historically, of course, we have been told to believe that this 'fall' from the grace of tradition was triggered by a profound change in the social role of the artist/architect after the middle of the eighteenth century. With the fall of the Church, the State and the aristocracy that had sustained him for centuries, the artist found himself confronted with an anonymous public. This new client, we are told, he despised. Paradoxically, however, the artist demanded the public's approval even when it could not understand his art. This nineteenth-century romantic attitude of the genius had much to do with the Modernist slogan 'down with conventions' and is still with us today, especially among the Neo-Modernist aesthetes.

But it is hardly possible to accept a view which imagines that a creative architect stares at a white board and designs *ex nihilo*. The empty sheet breeds a *horror vacui* and never a good idea. Human beings do *not* create in that way. Architecture may employ technology and it may be implicated with social and economic parameters; architects may read philosophy and novels and some may even be fascinated with fractal geometries and Boolean cubes, all of this is normal and human. But architecture is *not* made out of these things. Buildings can only be made out of other buildings. Architecture shapes itself. Its forms can no more exist outside architecture than the form of a sonata can exist outside music.

Any serious study of architecture (and art in general) soon shows that the real difference between the great and the lesser architect is that the former imitates the principles of a great heritage, unlike the latter who copies the mannerisms of his predecessors or of his contemporaries. That is the true meaning of creativity and tradition. But if creativity is to be understood as production *ex nihilo*, there would be no place for competence and intelligence. Even more, there would be no place for meaning.

It should be evident by now that an artist is said to be original exactly when he takes up the challenge of tradition and makes us see something more than we already know. In that sense artistic creativity elicits a sense of relevance from tradition. The creative artist makes us see the position we occupy within tradition; he raises both the question of the ontology of art and of its historicity.

Nowhere is this seen better than in the achievements of classical art and architecture. In fact, since the Hellenistic period, the concept of the classical has had both a normative (ontological) and a historical side. The normative side of the classical refers to the achievements of a particular stage in the development of mankind: namely, Greek Antiquity. What we call classical, in a normative sense, is that which endures the contingencies of a changing political and economic life and of taste and fashion.

But insofar as this norm points to the past accomplishments of a specific people and age, the idea of the classical always has a temporal side which gives it a historical dimension. This historical side of the classical is tied up with the awareness of 'anachronism': that is, with the awareness of a distance from the norm and a sense of loss. Dionysus of Halicarnassus was perhaps among the first to have felt such an acute sense of loss. His polemics

ABOVE: D Porphyrios, Paternoster Square Office Building and Central Tower, London, 1991; OPPOSITE: Sir John Vanbrugh, Blenheim Palace, Oxfordshire, 1704-20

against the vitiated rhetoric of the Hellenistic era recall the Renaissance polemics against Medieval retrogression, the eighteenth-century denouncement of Rococo as prurient as well as our twentieth-century criticism of the duplicity of Modernism. It is not by accident, therefore, that the concept of the classical was formulated for the first time in the later years of the Hellenistic period, exactly when deviation from the norm made the norm visible for the first time. Similarly, the stylistic concepts of Archaic and Gothic or of Mannerism and Baroque, all presuppose a relation to the normative concept of the classical. Gombrich understood this clearly when he wrote in *Norm and Form* that '. . . gothic (referred) to the not-yet-classical . . . and baroque to the no-longer-classical . . .'

It is because of such an articulation between the normative and the historical that we can say that every new humanism has no ground other than the modernity it helps to actualise. The classical accepts the contingent and the historical as elements that supply it with the necessary distance without which its project of demonstrating the continuity of human life would not be possible.

Ultimately, this articulation of the normative and the historical means that the classical is that which speaks of tradition in a modern voice thus highlighting man's capacity for millennial continuity. A work is classical not because its meaning is perpetuated but because it continually invites commentary and ferrets out the new. The classical reaches across culture and time and, taking the risk of anachronism, it heals the estrangement which humanism constantly faces. The classical, then, is certainly the enduring and timeless. But this timelessness always takes the form of modernity; that is, it takes the form of the relevance of tradition.

RIGHT: Otto Wagner, Stadtbahn Station at Karlsplatz, Vienna, c 1894-1901; OPPOSITE: Ictinus and Callicrates, Parthenon, Athens, c 447-432 BC

APPENDIX

PLATO

THE REPUBLIC

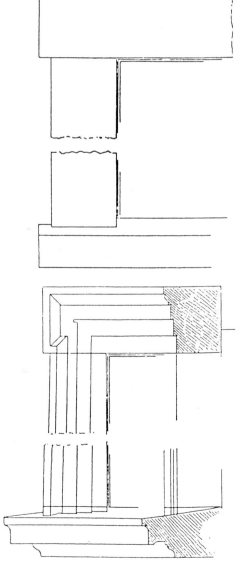

BOOK X

[. . .] 'What of the cabinet-maker? Were you not just now saying that he does not make the idea or form which we say is the real couch, the couch in itself, but only some particular couch?'

'Yes, I was.'

'Then if he does not make that which really is, he could not be said to make real being but something that resembles real being but is not that. But if anyone should say that being in the complete sense belongs to the work of the cabinet-maker or to that of any other handicraftsman, it seems that he would say what is not true.'

'That would be the view,' he said, 'of those who are versed in this kind of reasoning.' 'We must not be surprised, then, if this too is only a dim adumbration in comparison with reality.'

'No, we must not.'

'Shall we, then, use these very examples in our quest for the true nature of this imitator?' 'If you please,' he said.

'We get, then, these three couches, one, that in nature, which, I take it, we would say that God produces, or who else?'

'No one, I think.'

'And then there was one which the carpenter made.'

'Yes,' he said.

'And one which the painter. Is not that so?'

'So be it.'

'The painter, then, the cabinet-maker, and God, there are these three presiding over three kinds of couches.'

'Yes, three.'

'Now God, whether because he so willed or because some compulsion was laid upon him not to make more than one couch in nature, so wrought and created one only, the couch which really and in itself is. But two or more such were never created by God and never will come into being.'

'How so?' he said.

'Because,' said I, 'if he should make only two, there would again appear one of which they both would possess the form or idea, and that would be the couch that really is in and of itself, and not the other two.'

'Right,' he said. 'God, then, I take it, knowing this and wishing to be the real author of the couch that has real being and not of some particular couch, nor yet a particular cabinet-maker, produced it in nature unique.'

'So it seems.'

'Shall we, then, call him its true and natural begetter, or something of the kind?'

'That would certainly be right,' he said, 'since it is by and in nature that he has made this and all other things.'

'And what of the carpenter? Shall we not call him the creator of a couch?'

'Yes.'

'Shall we also say that the painter is the creator and maker of that sort of thing?'

'By no means.'

'What will you say he is in relation to the couch?'

'This,' said he, 'seems to me the most reasonable designation for him, that he is the imitator of the thing which those others produce.'

'Very good,' said I; 'the producer of the product three removes from nature you call the imitator?'

'By all means,' he said.

'This, then, will apply to the maker of tragedies also, if he is an imitator and is in his nature three removes from the king and the truth, as are all other imitators.'

'It would seem so.'

'We are in agreement, then, about the imitator. But tell me now this about the painter. Do you think that what he tries to imitate is in each case that thing itself in nature or the works of the craftsmen?'

'The works of the craftsmen,' he said.

'Is it the reality of them or the appearance? Define that further point.'

'What do you mean?' he said.

'This: Does a couch differ from itself according as you view it from the side or the front or in any other way? Or does it differ not at all in fact though it appears different, and so of other things?'

'That is the way of it,' he said; 'it appears other but differs not at all.'

'Consider, then, this very point. To which is painting directed in every case, to the imitation of reality as it is or of appearance as it appears? Is it an imitation of a phantasm or of the truth?'

'Of a phantasm,' he said.

'Then the mimetic art is far removed from truth, and this, it seems, is the reason why it can produce everything, because it touches or lays hold of only a small part of the object and that a phantom; as, for example, a painter, we say, will paint us a cobbler, a carpenter, and other craftsmen, though he himself has no expertness in any of these arts, but nevertheless if he were a good painter, by exhibiting at a distance his picture of a carpenter he would deceive children and foolish men, and make them believe it to be a real carpenter.'

'Why not?'

'But for all that, my friend, this, I take it, is what we ought to bear in mind in all such cases: When anyone reports to us of someone, that he has met a man who knows all the crafts and everything else that men severally know, and that there is nothing that he does not know more exactly than anybody else, our tacit rejoinder must be that he is a simple fellow, who apparently has met some magician or sleight-of-hand man and imitator and has been deceived by him into the belief that he is all-wise, because of his own inability to put to the proof and distinguish knowledge, ignorance and imitation.'

'Most true,' he said. [. . .]

'In heavens name, then, this business of imitation is concerned with the third remove from truth, is it not?'

'Yes.' [. . .]

'And the same things appear bent and straight to those who view them in water and out, or concave and convex, owing to similar errors of vision about colours, and there is obviously every confusion of this sort in our souls. And so scene-painting in its exploitation of this weakness of our nature falls nothing short of witchcraft, and so do jugglery and many other such contrivances.'

Plato, *The Republic*, Vol II, Books VI-X, translated by Paul Shorey, (William Heinemann, London and Harvard Univ Press, Cambridge, Massachusetts, MCMLXIII). Copyright Harvard Univ Press.

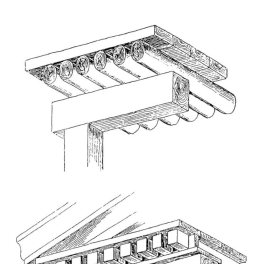

ABOVE AND OPPOSITE: The architrave imitates its post-and-lintel construction. The dentils are stylised representations of the joists. After C Uhde

PAGE 102: The Ecclesiasterion at Priene, c 200 BC
PAGE 103: Vase painting on a cylix depicting scenes from the Schools of Athens, early 5th century BC

ARISTOTLE
THE POETICS

I propose to treat of Poetry in itself and of its various kinds, noting the essential quality of each; to inquire into the structure of the plot as requisite to a good poem; into the number and nature of the parts of which a poem is composed; and similarly into whatever else falls within the same inquiry. Following, then, the order of nature, let us begin with the principles which come first.

Epic poetry and Tragedy, Comedy also and Dithyrambic poetry, and the music of the flute and of the lyre in most of their forms, are all in their general conception modes of imitation. They differ, however, from one another in three respects, – the medium, the objects, the manner or mode of imitation, being in each case distinct.

For as there are persons who, by conscious art or mere habit, imitate and represent various objects through the medium of colour and form, or again by the voice; so in the arts above mentioned, taken as a whole, the imitation is produced by rhythm, language, or 'harmony', either singly or combined. [. . .]

Such, then, are the differences of the arts with respect to the medium of imitation.

Since the objects of imitation are men in action, and these men must be either of a higher or a lower type (for moral character mainly answers to these divisions, goodness and badness being the distinguishing marks of moral differences), it follows that we must represent men either as better than in real life, or as worse, or as they are. It is the same in painting. Polygnotus depicted men as nobler than they are, Pauson as less noble, Dionysius drew them true to life. [. . .]

There is still a third difference – the manner in which each of these objects may be imitated. For the medium being the same, and the objects the same, the poet may imitate by narration – in which case he can either take another personality as Homer does, or speak in his own person, unchanged – or he may present all his characters as living and moving before us.

These, then, as we said at the beginning, are the three differences which distinguish artistic imitation – the medium, the objects, and the manner. [. . .]

This may suffice as to the number and nature of the various modes of imitation.

Poetry in general seems to have sprung from two causes, each of them lying deep in our nature. First, the instinct of imitation is implanted in man from childhood, one difference between him and other animals being that he is the most imitative of living creatures, and through imitation learns his earliest lessons; and no less universal is the pleasure felt in things imitated. We have evidence of this in the facts of experience. Objects which in themselves we view with pain, we delight to contemplate when reproduced with minute fidelity: such as the forms of the most ignoble animals and of dead bodies. The cause of this again is, that to learn gives the liveliest pleasure, not only to philosophers but to men in general; whose capacity, however, of learning is more limited. Thus the reason why men enjoy seeing a likeness is, that in contemplating it they find themselves learning or inferring, and saying perhaps, 'Ah, that is he.' For if you happen not to have seen the original, the pleasure will be due not to the imitation as such, but to the execution, the colouring, or some such other cause. [. . .]

Tragedy, then, is an imitation of an action that is serious, complete, and of a certain magnitude; in language embellished with each kind of artistic ornament, the several kinds being found in separate parts of the play; in the form of action, not of narrative; through pity and fear effecting the proper purgation of these emotions. By 'language embellished', I mean language into which rhythm, 'harmony', and song enter. By 'the several kinds in separate parts', I mean, that some parts are rendered through the medium of verse alone, others again with the aid of song. [. . .]

But most important of all is the structure of the incidents. For Tragedy is an imitation, not of men, but of an action and of life, and life consists in action, and its end is a mode of action, not a quality. Now character determines men's qualities, but it is by their actions that they are happy or the reverse. Dramatic action, therefore, is not with a view to the representation of character: character comes in as subsidiary to the actions. Hence the incidents and the plot are the end of a tragedy; and the end is the chief thing of all. Again, without action there cannot be a tragedy; there may be without character. The tragedies of most of our modern poets fail in the rendering of character; and of poets in general this is often true. It is the same in painting; and here lies the difference between Zeuxis and Polygnotus. Polygnotus delineates character well: the style of Zeuxis is devoid of ethical quality. Again, if you string together a set of speeches expressive of character, and well finished in point of diction and thought, you will not produce the essential tragic effect nearly so well as with a play which, however deficient in these respects, yet has a plot and artistically constructed incidents. [. . .]

These principles being established, let us now discuss the proper structure of the Plot, since this is the first and most important thing in Tragedy.

Now, according to our definition, Tragedy is an imitation of an action that is complete, and whole, and of a certain magnitude; for there may be a whole that is wanting in magnitude. A whole is that which has a beginning, a middle, and an end. A beginning is that which does not itself follow anything by causal necessity, but after which something naturally is or comes to be. An end, on the contrary, is that which itself naturally follows some other thing, either by necessity, or as a rule, but has nothing following it. A middle is that which follows something as some other thing follows it. A well constructed plot, therefore, must neither begin nor end at haphazard, but conform to these principles.

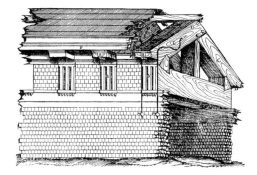

Again, a beautiful object, whether it be a living organism or any whole composed of parts, must not only have an orderly arrangement of parts, but must also be of a certain magnitude; for beauty depends on magnitude and order. Hence a very small animal organism cannot be beautiful; for the view of it is confused, the object being seen in an almost imperceptible moment of time. Nor, again, can one of vast size be beautiful, for as the eye cannot take it all in at once, the unity and sense of the whole is lost for the spectator; as for instance if there were one a thousand miles long. As, therefore, in the case of animate bodies and organisms a certain magnitude is necessary, and a magnitude which may be easily embraced in one view; so in the plot, a certain length is necessary, and a length which can be easily embraced by the memory. [. . .]

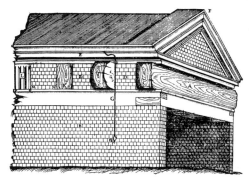

The poet being an imitator, like a painter or any other artist, must of necessity imitate one of three objects – things as they were or are, things as they are said or thought to be, or things as they ought to be. [. . .]

SH Butcher, *Aristotle's Theory of Poetry and Fine Art*, with a critical text and translation of *The Poetics*, (Dover Publications, New York, 4th edition, 1951).

ABOVE AND OPPOSITE: Architecture as the imitation of building construction, after Giovanantonio Rusconi, Della Architettura, 1590

HORACE
THE ART OF POETRY

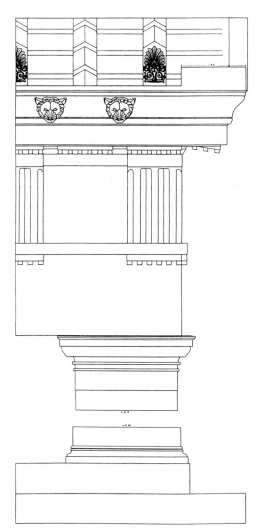

If in a picture, Piso, you should see
A handsome woman with a fish's tail,
Or a man's head upon a horse's neck,
Or limbs of beasts of the most diff'rent kinds,
Cover'd with feathers of all sorts of birds,
Would you not laugh, and think the painter mad?
Trust me, that book is as ridiculous,
Whose incoherent style (like sick men's dreams)
Varies all shapes, and mixes all extremes.
Painters and poets have been still allow'd
Their pencils, and their fancies, unconfin'd.
This privilege we freely give and take;
But nature; and the common laws of sense
Forbid to reconcile antipathies,
Or make a snake engender with a dove,
And hungry tigers court the tender lambs.

Some that at first have promis'd mighty things,
Applaud themselves, when a few florid lines
Shine through th' insipid dullness of the rest;
Here they describe a temple, or a wood,
Or streams that through delightful meadows run,
And there the rainbow, or the rapid Rhine,
But they misplace them all, and crowd them in,
And are as much to seek in other things,
As he, that only can design a tree,
Would be to draw a shipwreck or a storm.
When you begin with so much pomp and show;
Why is the end so little and so mean?
Be what you will, so you be still the same.

Most poets fall into the grossest faults,
Deluded by a seeming excellence:
In striving to be short, they grow obscure;
And when they would write smoothly, they want strength,
Their spirits sink; while others that affect
A lofty style, swell to a tympany,
Some tim'rous wretches start at ev'ry blast,
And fearing tempests, dare not leave the shore;
Others, in love with wild variety,
Draw boars in waves, and dolphins in a wood;

Thus fear of erring, join'd with want of skill,
Is a most certain way of erring still.

The meanest workman in th' Aemilian square,
May grave the nails, or imitate the hair,
But cannot finish what he hath begun;
What is there more ridiculous than he?
For one or two good features in a face,
Where all the rest are scandalously ill,
Make it but more remarkably deform'd,

Let poets match their subject to their strength,
And often try what weight they can support,
And what their shoulders are too weak to bear.
After a serious and judicious choice,
Method and eloquence will never fail. [. . .]

If your bold muse dare tread unbeaten paths,
And bring new characters upon the stage,
Be sure you keep them up to their first height.
New subjects are not easily explain'd,
And you had better choose a well-known theme,
Than trust to an invention of your own; [. . .]
But then you must not copy trivial things,
Nor word for word too faithfully translate,
Nor (as some servile imitators do)
Prescribe at first such strict uneasy rules,
As they must ever slavishly observe,
Or all the laws of decency renounce. [. . .]

Sound judgment is the ground of writing well:
And when philosophy directs your choice
To proper subjects rightly understood,
Words from your pen will naturally flow;
He only gives the proper characters,
Who knows the duty of all ranks of men,
And what we owe to country, parents, friends,
How judges, and how senators should act,
And what becomes a general to do;
Those are the likest copies, which are drawn
By the original of human life.

Poems, like pictures, are of diff'rent sorts,
Some better at a distance, others near,
Some love the dark, some choose the clearest light,
And boldly challenge the most piercing eye,
Some please for once, some will for ever please.

The Complete Works of Horace, translated by various
hands, (JM Dent & Sons, London and EP Dutton &
Co, New York, 1953). Copyright Everyman's Library Ltd.

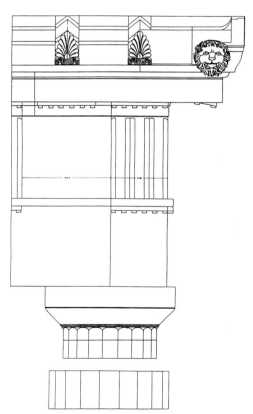

*ABOVE: Propylaea of Eleusis, Doric order, after JJ
Hittorff,* Les antiquités de l'Attique, *1832; OPPO-
SITE: The Temple of Diana in Eleusis, the order of
the antae, after JJ Hittorff*

CICERO
ON INVENTION

BOOK I

I have often seriously debated with myself whether men and communities have received more good or evil from oratory and a consuming devotion to eloquence. For when I ponder the troubles in our commonwealth, and run over in my mind the ancient misfortunes of mighty cities, I see that no little part of the disasters was brought about by men of eloquence. When, on the other hand, I begin to search in the records of literature for events which occurred before the period which our generation can remember, I find that many cities have been founded, that the flames of a multitude of wars have been extinguished, and that the strongest alliances and most sacred friendships have been formed not only by the use of the reason but also more easily by the help of eloquence. For my own part, after long thought, I have been led by reason itself to hold this opinion first and foremost, that wisdom without eloquence does too little for the good of states, but that eloquence without wisdom is generally highly disadvantageous and is never helpful. Therefore if anyone neglects the study of philosophy and moral conduct, which is the highest and most honourable of pursuits, and devotes his whole energy to the practice of oratory, his civic life is nurtured into something useless to himself and harmful to his country; but the man who equips himself with the weapons of eloquence, not to be able to attack the welfare of his country but to defend it, he, I think, will be a citizen most helpful and most devoted both to his own interests and those of his community.

Moreover, if we wish to consider the origin of this thing we call eloquence – whether it be an art, a study, a skill, or a gift of nature – we shall find that it arose from most honourable causes and continued on its way from the best of reasons. For there was a time when men wandered at large in the fields like animals and lived on wild fare; they did nothing by the guidance of reason, but relied chiefly on physical strength; there was as yet no ordered system of religious worship nor of social duties; no one had seen legitimate marriage nor had they learned the advantages of an equitable code of law. And so through their ignorance and error blind and unreasoning passion satisfied itself by misuse of bodily strength, which is a very dangerous servant.

At this juncture a man – great and wise I am sure – became aware of the power latent in man and the wide field offered by his mind for great achievements if one could develop this power and improve it by instruction. Men were scattered in the fields and hidden in sylvan retreats when he assembled and gathered them in accordance with a plan; he introduced them to every useful and honourable occupation, though they cried out against it at first because of its novelty, and then when through reason and eloquence they had listened with greater attention, he transformed them from wild savages into a kind and gentle folk.

To me, at least, it does not seem possible that a mute and voiceless wisdom could have turned men suddenly from their habits and introduced them to different

OPPOSITE: Vernacular buildings in Patmos

patterns of life. Consider another point; after cities had been established how could it have been brought to pass that men should learn to keep faith and observe justice and become accustomed to obey others voluntarily and believe not only that they must work for the common good but even sacrifice life itself, unless men had been able by eloquence to persuade their fellows of the truth of what they had discovered by reason? Certainly only a speech at the same time powerful and entrancing could have induced one who had great physical strength to submit to justice without violence, so that he suffered himself to be put on a par with those among whom he could excel, and abandoned voluntarily a most agreeable custom, especially since this custom had already acquired through lapse of time the force of a natural right.

*   *   *

This was the way in which at first eloquence came into being and advanced to greater development, and likewise afterward in the greatest undertakings of peace and war it served the highest interests of mankind. But when a certain agreeableness of manner – a depraved imitation of virtue – acquired the power of eloquence unaccompanied by any consideration of moral duty, then low cunning supported by talent grew accustomed to corrupt cities and undermine the lives of men.

Let me now set forth the origin of this evil also, since I have explained the beginning of the good done by eloquence. It seems to me very probable that there was a time when those who lacked eloquence and wisdom were not accustomed to meddle with public affairs, and when on the other hand great and eloquent men did not concern themselves with private suits at law, but while matters of the greatest importance were managed by men of the highest distinction, there were, I think, other men not without shrewdness who concerned themselves with the petty disputes of private citizens. Since in these disputes men grew accustomed to stand on the side of falsehood against the truth, constant practice in speaking led them to assume a bold front; the inevitable result was that the better class was compelled because of injuries to their fellow citizens to resist the audacious and help their own kin and friends. And so, because one who had acquired eloquence alone to the neglect of the study of philosophy often appeared equal in power of speech and sometimes even superior, such a one seemed in his own opinion and that of the mob to be fit to govern the state. Therefore it was not undeserved, I am sure, that whenever rash and audacious men had taken the helm of the ship of state great and disastrous wrecks occurred. These events brought eloquence into such odium and unpopularity that men of the greatest talent left a life of strife and tumult for some quiet pursuit, as sailors seek refuge in port from a raging storm. For this reason, I think, at a later period the other worthy and honourable studies were prosecuted vigorously in quiet seclusion by the men of highest virtue and were brought to a brilliant development, while this study of eloquence was abandoned by most of them and fell into disuse at a time when it needed to be maintained more earnestly and extended with greater effort. For the more shamefully an honourable and worthy profession was abused by the folly and audacity of dull-witted and unprincipled men with the direst consequences to the state, the more earnestly should the better citizens have put up a resistance to them and taken thought for the welfare of the republic. [. . .]

BOOK II

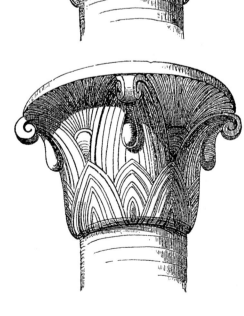

The citizens of Croton, once upon a time, when they had abundant wealth and were numbered among the most prosperous in Italy, desired to enrich with distinguished paintings the temple of Juno, which they held in the deepest veneration. They, therefore, paid a large fee to Zeuxis of Heraclea who was considered at that time to excel all other artists, and secured his services for their project. He painted many panels, some of which have been preserved to the present by the sanctity of the shrine; he also said that he wished to paint a picture of Helen so that the portrait though silent and lifeless might embody the surpassing beauty of womanhood. This delighted the Crotoniats, who had often heard that he surpassed all others in the portrayal of women. For they thought that if he exerted himself in the genre in which he was supreme, he would leave an outstanding work of art in that temple. Nor were they mistaken in this opinion. For Zeuxis immediately asked them what girls they had of surpassing beauty. They took him directly to the wrestling school and showed him many very handsome young men. For at one time the men of Croton excelled all in strength and beauty of body, and brought home the most glorious victories in athletic contests with the greatest distinction. As he was greatly admiring the handsome bodies, they said, 'There are in our city the sisters of these men; you may get an idea of their beauty from these youths.' 'Please send me then the most beautiful of these girls, while I am painting the picture that I have promised, so that the true beauty may be transferred from the living model to the mute likeness.' Then the citizens of Croton by a public decree assembled the girls in one place and allowed the painter to choose whom he wished. He selected five, whose names many poets recorded because they were approved by the judgement of him who must have been the supreme judge of beauty. He chose five because he did not think all the qualities which he sought to combine in a portrayal of beauty could be found in one person, because in no single case has Nature made anything perfect and finished in every part. Therefore, as if she would have no bounty to lavish on the others if she gave everything to one, she bestows some advantage on one and some on another, but always joins with it some defect.

*   *   *

In a similar fashion when the inclination arose in my mind to write a textbook of rhetoric, I did not set before myself some one model which I thought necessary to reproduce in all details, of whatever sort they might be, but after collecting all the works on the subject I excerpted what seemed the most suitable precepts from each, and so culled the flower of many minds. For each of the writers who are worthy of fame and reputation seemed to say something better than anyone else, but not to attain pre-eminence in all points. It seemed folly therefore, either to refuse to follow the good ideas of any author, merely because I was offended by some fault in his work, or to follow the mistakes of a writer who had attracted me by some correct precept. And it is also true of other pursuits that if men would choose the most appropriate contributions from many sources rather than devote themselves unreservedly to one leader only, they would offend less by arrogance, they would not be so obstinate in wrong courses, and would suffer somewhat less from ignorance. And if my knowledge of the art of rhetoric had equalled his knowledge of painting, perhaps this work of mine might be more famous in its class than he is in his painting. For I had a larger number of models to choose from than he had. He could choose from one city and from the group of girls who were alive at that time, but I was able to set out before me the store of wisdom of all who had written from the very beginning of instruction in rhetoric down to the present time, and choose whatever was acceptable. [. . .]

Cicero, *De Inventione, De Optimo Genere Oratorum, Topica*, translated by HM Hubbell (William Heinemann, London and Harvard University Press, Cambridge, Mass, MCMLXXVI). Copyright Harvard University Press.

ABOVE: Capitals from the Bacchus Theatre in Athens and the Temple of Apollo at Phigaleia, after J Durm; OPPOSITE: Egyptian capitals from Thebes, 1250 BC, after J Durm

PLINY
NATURAL HISTORY

BOOK XXXV

[. . .] Parrhasius, it is recorded, entered into a competition with Zeuxis, who produced a picture of grapes so successfully represented that birds flew up to the stage-buildings; whereupon Parrhasius himself produced such a realistic picture of a curtain that Zeuxis, proud of the verdict of the birds, requested that the curtain should now be drawn and the picture displayed; and when he realised his mistake, with a modesty that did him honour he yielded up the prize, saying that whereas he had deceived birds Parrhasius had deceived him, an artist. It is said that Zeuxis also subsequently painted a Child Carrying Grapes, and when birds flew to the fruit with the same frankness as before he strode up to the picture in anger with it and said, 'I have painted the grapes better than the child, as if I had made a success of that as well, the birds would inevitably have been afraid of it.' [. . .]

A clever incident took place between Protogenes and Apelles. Protogenes lived at Rhodes, and Apelles made the voyage there from a desire to make himself acquainted with Protogenes' works, as that artist was hitherto only known to him by reputation. He went at once to his studio. The artist was not there but there was a panel of considerable size on the easel prepared for painting, which was in the charge of a single old woman. In answer to his enquiry, she told him that Protogenes was not at home, and asked who it was she should report as having wished to see him. 'Say it was this person,' said Apelles, and taking up a brush he painted in colour across the panel an extremely fine line; and when Protogenes returned the old woman showed him what had taken place. The story goes that the artist, after looking closely at the finish of this, said that the new arrival was Apelles, as so perfect a piece of work tallied with nobody else; and he himself, using another colour, drew a still finer line exactly on the top of the first one, and leaving the room told the attendant to show it to the visitor if he returned and add that this was the person he was in search of; and so it happened; for Apelles came back, and, ashamed to be beaten, cut the lines with another in a third colour, leaving no room for any further display of minute work. Hereupon Protogenes admitted he was defeated, and flew down to the harbour to look for the visitor; and he decided that the panel should be handed on to posterity as it was, to be admired as a marvel by everybody, but particularly by artists. I am informed that it was burnt in the first fire which occurred in Caesar's palace on the Palatine; it had been previously much admired by us, on its vast surface containing nothing else than the almost invisible lines, so that among the outstanding works of many artists it looked like a blank space, and by that very fact attracted attention and was more esteemed than any masterpiece.

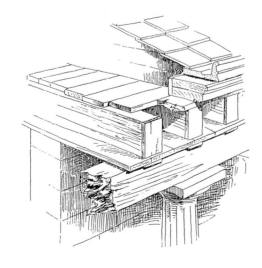

Moreover it was a regular custom with Apelles never to let a day of business to be so fully occupied that he did not practise his art by drawing a line, which has passed from him into a proverb. Another habit of his was when he had finished his works to place them in a gallery in the view of passers by, and he himself stood out of sight behind the picture and listened to hear what faults were noticed, rating the public as a more observant critic than himself. And it is said that he was found fault with by a shoemaker because in drawing a subject's sandals he had represented the loops in them as one too few, and the next day the same critic was so proud of the artist's correcting the fault indicated by his previous objection that he found fault with the leg, but Apelles indignantly looked out from behind the picture and rebuked him, saying that a shoemaker in his criticism must not go beyond the sandal – a remark that has also passed into a proverb. [. . .]

Pliny, *Natural History*, Volume IX, Libri XXXIII-XXXV, translated by H Rackham (William Heinemann, London and Harvard University Press, Cambridge, Mass, MCMLXVIII). Copyright Harvard University Press.

LEFT: Tomb of Absalom, Jerusalem, c 50 AD; OPPOSITE: Timber construction of Doric temple, after C Uhde

VITRUVIUS
ON ARCHITECTURE

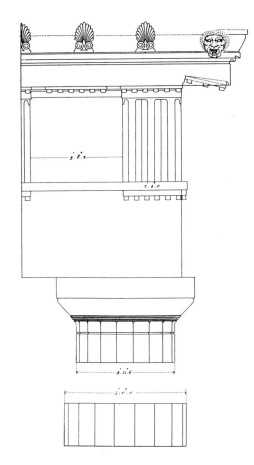

BOOK I
CHAPTER II
Of What Things Architecture Consists

1 Now architecture consists of Order, which in Greek is called *taxis*, and of Arrangement, which the Greeks name *diathesis*, and of Proportion and Symmetry and Decor and Distribution which in Greek is called *oeconomia*.

2 Order is the balanced adjustment of the details of the work separately, and, as to the whole, the arrangement of the proportion with a view to a symmetrical result. This is made up of Dimension, which in Greek is called *posotes*. Now Dimension is the taking of modules from the parts of the work; and the suitable effect of the whole work arising from the several subdivisions of the parts.

Arrangement, however, is the fit assemblage of details, and, arising from this assemblage, the elegant effect of the work and its dimensions, along with a certain quality or character. The kinds of the arrangement (which in Greek are called *ideae*) are these: ichnography (plan); orthography (elevation); scenography (perspective). Ichnography (plan) demands the competent use of compass and rule; by these plans are laid out upon the sites provided. Orthography (elevation), however, is the vertical image of the front, and a figure slightly tinted to show the lines of the future work. Scenography (perspective) also is the shading of the front and the retreating sides, and the correspondence of all lines to the vanishing point, which is the centre of a circle. These three (plan, elevation and perspective) arise from imagination and invention. Imagination rests upon the attention directed with minute and observant fervour to the charming effect proposed. Invention, however, is the solution of obscure problems; the treatment of a new undertaking disclosed by an active intelligence. Such are the outlines of Arrangement.

3 Proportion implies a graceful semblance; the suitable display of details in their context. This is attained when the details of the work are of a height suitable to their breadth, of a breadth suitable to their length; in a word, when everything has a symmetrical correspondence.

4 Symmetry also is the appropriate harmony arising out of the details of the work itself; the correspondence of each given detail among the separate details to the form of the design as a whole. As in the human body, from cubit, foot, palm, inch and other small parts comes the symmetric quality of eurhythmy; so is it in the completed building. First, in sacred buildings, either from the thickness of columns, or a triglyph, or the module; of a balista by the perforation which the Greeks call *peritreton*; by the space between the rowlocks in a ship which is called *dipechyaia*: so also the calculation of symmetries, in the case of other works, is found from the details.

5 Decor demands the faultless ensemble of a work composed, in accordance with precedent, of approved details. It obeys convention, which in Greek is called *thematismos*, or custom or nature. Convention is obeyed when buildings are put up

in the open and hypethral to Jupiter of the Lightning, to Heaven, the Sun, the Moon; for of these gods, both the appearance and effect we see present in the open, the world of light. To Minerva, Mars and Hercules, Doric temples will be built; for to these gods, because of their might, buildings ought to be erected without embellishments. Temples designed in the Corinthian style will seem to have details suited to Venus, Flora, Proserpine, Fountains, Nymphs; for to these goddesses, on account of their gentleness, works constructed with slighter proportions and adorned with flowers, foliage, spirals and volutes will seem to gain in a just decor. To Juno, Diana and Father Bacchus, and the other gods who are of the same likeness, if Ionic temples are erected, account will be taken of their middle quality; because the determinate character of their temples will avoid the severe manner of the Doric and the softer manner of the Corinthian.

6 With reference to fashion, decor is thus expressed; when to magnificent interiors vestibules also are made harmonious and elegant. For if the interior apartments present an elegant appearance, while the approaches are low and uncomely, they will not be accompanied by fitness. Again, if, in Doric entablatures, dentils are carved on the cornices, or if with voluted capitals and Ionic entablatures, triglyphs are applied, characteristics are transferred from one style to another: the work as a whole will jar upon us, since it includes details foreign to the order.

7 There will be a natural decor: first, if for all temples there shall be chosen the most healthy sites with suitable springs in those places in which shrines are to be set up; secondly and especially for Aesculapius and Salus; and generally for those gods by whose medical power sick persons are manifestly healed. For when sick persons are moved from a pestilent to a healthy place and the water supply is from wholesome fountains, they will more quickly recover. So will it happen that the divinity (from the nature of the site) will gain a greater and higher reputation and authority. [. . .]

BOOK I
CHAPTER III

2 [. . .] Now these should be so carried out that account is taken of strength, utility, grace. Account will be taken of *strength* when the foundations are carried down to the solid ground, and when from each material there is a choice of supplies without parsimony; of *utility*, when the sites are arranged without mistake and impediment to their use, and a fit and convenient disposition for the aspect of each kind; of *grace*, when the appearance of the work shall be pleasing and elegant, and the scale of the constituent parts is justly calculated for symmetry.

BOOK II
CHAPTER I
The Origin Of Building

1 Men, in the old way, were born like animals in forests and caves and woods, and passed their life feeding on the food of the fields. Meanwhile, once upon a time, in a certain place, trees, thickly crowded, tossed by storms and winds and rubbing their branches together, kindled a fire. Terrified by the raging flame, those who were about that place were put to flight. Afterwards when the thing was quieted down, approaching nearer they perceived that the advantage was great for their bodies from the heat of the fire. They added fuel, and keeping it up, they brought others; and pointing it out by signs they showed what advantages they had from it. In this concourse of mankind, when sounds were variously uttered by the breath, by daily custom they fixed words as they had chanced to come. Then, indicating things more frequently and by habit, they came by chance to speak according to the event, and so they generated conversation with one another.

2 Therefore, because of the discovery of fire, there arose at the beginning,

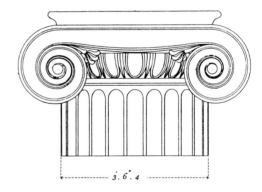

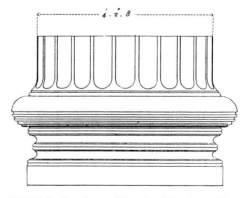

ABOVE: *Ionic column of Temple of Bacchus at Teos, after W Wilkins,* The Civil Architecture of Vitruvius, *1812; OPPOSITE: Doric order of the Propylaea in Athens, after W Wilkins*

concourse among men, deliberation and a life in common. Many came together into one place, having from nature this boon beyond other animals, that they should walk, not with head down, but upright, and should look upon the magnificence of the world and of the stars. They also easily handled with their hands and fingers whatever they wished. Hence after thus meeting together, they began, some to make shelters of leaves, some to dig caves under the hills, some to make of mud and wattles places for shelter, imitating the nests of swallows and their methods of building. Then observing the houses of others and adding to their ideas new things from day to day, they produced better kinds of huts.

3 Since men were of an imitative and teachable nature, they boasted of their inventions as they daily showed their various achievements in building, and thus, exercising their talents in rivalry, were rendered of better judgment daily. And first, with upright forked props and twigs put between, they wove their walls. Others made walls, drying moistened clods which they bound with wood, and covered with reeds and leafage, so as to escape the rain and heat. When in winter-time the roofs could not withstand the rains, they made ridges, and smearing clay down the sloping roofs, they drew off the rain-water.

4 That these things were so practised from the beginnings above described we can observe, seeing that to this day buildings are constructed for foreign nations of these materials, as in Gaul, Spain, Portugal, Aquitaine, with oak shingles or thatch. In Pontus among the nation of the Colchi, because of their rich forests, two whole trees are laid flat, right and left, on the ground, a space being left between them as wide as the lengths of the trees allow. On the furthest parts of them, two others are placed transversely, and these four trees enclose in the middle the space for the dwelling. Then, laying upon them alternate beams from the four sides, they join up the angles. And so constructing the walls with trees, they raise up towers rising perpendicular from the lowest parts. The gaps which are left by the thickness of the timber they block up with splinters and clay. Further, they raise the roofs by cutting off the cross-beams at the end and gradually narrowing them. And so, from the four sides they raise over the middle a pyramid on high. This they cover with leafage and clay, and, barbarian fashion, construct the coved roofs of their towers.

5 But the Phrygians, who are dwellers in the plains, owing to the absence of forests, lack timber. Hence they choose natural mounds, and dividing them in the middle by a trench and digging tracks through, open out spaces as far as the nature of the place allows. They fasten logs together at the upper end, and so make pyramids. These they cover with reeds and brushwood and pile up very large hillocks from the ground above their dwellings. This arrangement of their dwellings makes the winter quite warm, and the summer cool. Some construct covered huts from the sedge of the marshes. Among other nations, also, in many places, the erection of huts is carried out in a parallel and similar manner. Not less also at Marseilles we can observe roofs without tiles, made of earth and kneaded with straw. At Athens there is an ancient type of building, on the Areopagus, to this day covered with mud. Also in the Capitolium the Hut of Romulus, and in the Citadel, shrines covered with straw, can remind us, and signify the customs and the antiquities of Rome.

6 Thus by these examples we can infer concerning the ancient invention of buildings, reasoning that they were similar.

When, however, by daily work men had rendered their hands more hardened for building, and by practising their clever talents they had by habit acquired craftsmanship, then also the industry, which rooted itself in their minds, caused those who were more eager herein to profess themselves craftsmen. When, therefore, these matters were so first ordained and Nature had not only equipped the human races with perceptions like other animals, but also had armed their minds with ideas and purposes, and had put the other animals under their power, then from the construction of buildings they progressed by degrees to other crafts and disciplines, and they led the way from a savage and rustic life to a peaceful civilisation.

7 Then, building up themselves in spirit, and looking out and forward with larger ideas born from the variety of their crafts, they began to build, not huts, but houses, on foundations, and with brick walls, or built of stone; and with roofs of wood and tiles. Then by the observations made in their studies they were led on from wandering and uncertain judgments to the assured method of symmetry. [. . .]

BOOK III
CHAPTER I
The Planning Of Temples

1 [. . .] Proportion consists in taking a fixed module, in each case, both for the parts of a building and for the whole, by which the method of symmetry is put into practice. For without symmetry and proportion no temple can have a regular plan; that is, it must have an exact proportion worked out after the fashion of the members of a finely-shaped human body.

2 For Nature has so planned the human body that the face from the chin to the top of the forehead and the roots of the hair is a tenth part; also the palm of the hand from the wrist to the top of the middle finger is as much; the head from the chin to the crown, an eighth part; from the top of the breast with the bottom of the neck to the roots of the hair, a sixth part; from the middle of the breast to the crown, a fourth part; a third part of the height of the face is from the bottom of the chin to the bottom of the nostrils; the nose from the bottom of the nostrils to the line between the brows, as much; from that line to the roots of the hair, the forehead is given as a third part. The foot is a sixth of the height of the body; the cubit a quarter, the breast also a quarter. The other limbs also have their own proportionate measurements. And by using these, ancient painters and famous sculptors have attained great and unbounded distinction.

3 In like fashion the members of temples ought to have dimensions of their several parts answering suitably to the general sum of their whole magnitude. Now the navel is naturally the exact centre of the body. For if a man lies on his back with hands and feet outspread, and the centre of a circle is placed on his navel, his figure and toes will be touched by the circumference. Also a square will be found described within the figure, in the same way as a round figure is produced. For if we measure from the sole of the foot to the top of the head, and apply the measure to the outstretched hands, the breadth will be found equal to the height, just like sites which are squared by rule.

4 Therefore if Nature has planned the human body so that the members correspond in their proportions to its complete configuration, the ancients seem to have had reason in determining that in the execution of their works they should observe an exact adjustment of the several members to the general pattern of the plan. Therefore, since in all their works they handed down orders, they did so especially in building temples, the excellences and the faults of which usually endure for ages.

5 Moreover, they collected from the members of the human body the proportionate dimensions which appear necessary in all building operations; the finger or inch, the palm, the foot, the cubit. And these they grouped into the perfect number which the Greeks call *teleon*. [. . .]

Vitruvius, *On Architecture*, Vol I, translated by Frank Granger (William Heinemann, London and Harvard University Press, Cambridge, Mass, MCMLXXXIII). Copyright Harvard Univ Press.

ABOVE: Vestibule to Peribolus of Eleusis, capital of the antae, side view, after JJ Hittorff; OPPOSITE: Corinthian order of a choragic monument in Athens, after W Wilkins

ALBERTI
TEN BOOKS ON ARCHITECTURE

BOOK I
CHAPTER IX
Of the Compartition, and of the Origin of Building.

The whole force of the invention and all our skill and knowledge in the art of building, is required in the compartition because the distinct parts of the entire building, and, to use such a word, the entireness of each of those parts, and the union and agreement of all the lines and angles in the work, duly ordered for convenience, pleasure and beauty, are disposed and measured out by the compartition alone: for if a city, according to the opinion of philosophers, be no more than a great house, and, on the other hand, a house be a little city; why may it not be said, that the members of that house are so many little houses; such as the courtyard, the hall, the parlour, the portico, and the like? And what is there in any of these, which, if omitted by carelessness or negligence, will not greatly take from the praise and dignity of the work. Great care and diligence therefore is to be used in well considering these things, which so much concern the whole building; and in so ordering it, that even the most inconsiderable parts may not be unconformable to the rules of art and good contrivance. What has been already said above of the region and platform, may be of no small use in doing of this aptly and conveniently; and as the members of the body are correspondent to each other, so it is fit that one part should answer to another in a building; whence we say, that great edifices require great members. Which indeed was so well observed by the ancients, that they used much larger bricks, as well as other materials, about public and large buildings than in private ones. To every member therefore ought to be allotted its fit place and proper situation; not less than dignity requires, not greater than conveniency demands; not in an impertinent or indecent place, but in a situation so proper to itself, that it could be set nowhere else more fitly. Nor should the part of the structure, that is to be of the greatest honour, be thrown into a remote corner; nor that which ought to be the most public, into a private hole; nor that which should be most private, be set in too conspicuous a place. We should besides have regard to the seasons of the year, and make a great deal of difference between hot places and cold, both in proportions and situation. If rooms for summer are large and spacious, and those for winter more compact, it will not be at all amiss; the summer ones shady and open to the air, and the winter ones to the sun. And here we should provide, that the inhabitants may not be obliged to pass out of a cold place into a hot one, without a medium of temperate air; or out of a warm one into one exposed to cold and winds; because nothing is so prejudicial to human bodies. And these ought to agree one member with another to perfect and compose the main design and beauty of the whole; that we may not so lay out our whole study in adorning one part, as to leave the rest neglected and homely in comparison of it; but let them bear that proportion among themselves, that they may appear to be an entire and perfect body, and not disjointed and unfinished members.

OPPOSITE: Church in Ubeda, c 16th century

Moreover in the forming of these members too, we ought to imitate the modesty of nature; because in this, as well as in other cases, the world never commends a moderation, so much as it blames an extravagant intemperance in building. Let the members therefore be modestly proportioned, and necessary for your uses. For all building in general, if you consider it well, owes its birth to necessity, was nursed by convenience and embellished by use; pleasure was the last thing consulted in it, which is never truly obtained by things that are immoderate. Let your building therefore be such that it may not want any members which it has not, and that those which it has, may not in any respect deserve to be condemned. Nor would I have the edifice terminated all the way with even continued lines void of all manner of variety; for some please us by their largeness, others with being little, and others moderate. One part therefore should be terminated with straight lines, another with curve, and another again with straight and curve mixed together; provided you observe the caution I have so often given you, to avoid falling into the error of excess, so as to seem to have made a monster with limbs disproportionable: variety is without dispute a very great beauty in everything, when it joins and brings together, in a regular manner, things different but proportionable to each other; but it is rather shocking, if they are unsuitable and incoherent. For as in music, when the bass answers the treble and the tenor agrees with both, there arises from that variety of sounds an harmonious and wonderful union of proportions which delights and enchants our senses; so the like happens in everything else that strikes and pleases our fancy. Lastly these things must be so executed, as use or convenience requires, or according to the approved practice of men of skill; because deviating from established custom, generally robs a thing of its whole beauty, as conforming to it, is applauded and attended with success. Nevertheless, although other famous architects seem, by their practice, to have determined this or that compartition, whether *Doric,* or *Ionic,* or *Corinthian,* or *Tuscan,* to be the most convenient of any; yet they do not thereby tie us down to follow them so closely, as to transcribe their very designs into this work of ours; but only stir us up by their instructions to produce something of our own invention, and to endeavour to acquire equal or greater praise than they did. [. . .]

BOOK II
CHAPTER II
That we ought to undertake nothing above our Abilities, nor strive against Nature, and that we ought also not only to consider what we can do, but what is fit for us to do, and in what Place it is that we are to build.

On examining your model, among other points to be considered, you must take care not to forget these. First, not to undertake a thing, which is above the power of man to do, and not to pretend to strive directly contrary to the nature of things. For nature, if you force or wrest her out of her way, whatever strength you may do it with, will yet in the end overcome and break through all opposition and hindrance; and the most obstinate violence (to use such an expression) will at last be forced to yield to her daily and continual perseverance assisted by length of time. How many of the mighty works of men do we read of, and know ourselves to have been destroyed by no other cause than that they contended against nature? Who does not laugh at him, that having made a bridge upon ships, intended to ride over the sea? Or rather, who does not hate him for his folly and insolence? The haven of *Claudius* below *Ostia,* and that of *Hadrian* near *Terracina,* works in all other respects likely to last to eternity, yet now having their mouths stopped with sand, and their beds quite chocked up, they have been long since totally destroyed by the continual assaults of the sea, which incessantly washing against it gains from it daily. What then think ye will happen in any place where you pretend to oppose or entirely repel the violence of water, or the enormous weights of rocks tumbling

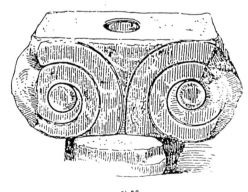

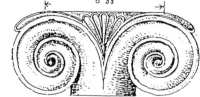

down on you in ruins? This being considered, we ought never to undertake anything that is not exactly agreeable to nature; and moreover we should take care not to enter upon a work in which we may be so much wanting to ourselves as to be forced to leave it imperfect. [. . .]

CHAPTER V
BOOK IX
That the beauty of all edifices arises principally from three things, namely, the Number, Figure and Collocation of the several members.

[. . .] But the judgment which you make that a thing is beautiful, does not proceed from mere opinion, but from a secret argument and discourse implanted in the mind itself; which plainly appears to be so from this, that no man beholds anything ugly or deformed, without an immediate hatred and abhorrence. Whence this sensation of the mind arises, and how it is formed, would be a question too subtle for this place: however, let us consider and examine it from those things which are obvious, and make more immediately to the subject in hand: for without question there is a certain excellence and natural beauty in the figures and forms of buildings, which immediately strike the mind with pleasure and admiration. It is my opinion, that beauty, majesty, gracefulness, and the like charms, consist in those particulars which if you alter or take away, the whole would be made homely and disagreeable. If we are convinced of this, it can be no very tedious enquiry to consider those things which may be taken away, increased or altered, especially in figures and forms: for everybody consists of certain peculiar parts, of which if you take away any one, or lessen or enlarge it, or remove it to an improper place; that which before gave the beauty and grace to this body would at once be lamed and spoiled. From hence we may conclude, to avoid prolixity in this research, that there are three things principally in which the whole of what we are looking into consists: the Number and that which I have called the Finishing, and the Collocation. But there is still something else besides, which arises from the conjunction and connection of these other parts, and gives the beauty and grace to the whole: which we call Congruity, which we may consider as the original of all that is graceful and handsome. The business and office of congruity is to put together members differing from each other in their natures, in such a manner that they may conspire to form a beautiful whole: so that whenever such a composition offers itself to the mind either by the conveyance of the sight, hearing or any of the other senses, we immediately perceive this congruity; for by nature we desire things perfect, and adhere to them with pleasure when they are offered to us; nor does this congruity arise so much from the body in which it is found, or any of its members, as from itself, and from nature, so that its true seat is in the mind and in reason; and accordingly it has a very large field to exercise itself and flourish in, and runs through every part and action of man's life, and every production of nature herself, which are all directed by the law of congruity, nor does nature study anything more than to make all her works absolute and perfect, which they could never be without this congruity, since they would want that consent of parts which is so necessary to perfection. But we need not say more upon this point, and if what we have here laid down appears to be true, we may conclude beauty to be such a consent and agreement of the parts of a whole in which it is found, as to number, finishing and collocation, as congruity, that is to say, the principal law of nature requires. This is what architecture chiefly aims at, and by this she obtains her beauty, dignity and value. The ancients knowing from the nature of things that the matter was in fact, as I have here stated it, and being convinced that if they neglected this main point they should never produce anything great or commendable, did in their works propose to themselves chiefly the imitation of nature, as the greatest artist at all manner of compositions; and for this purpose they laboured, as

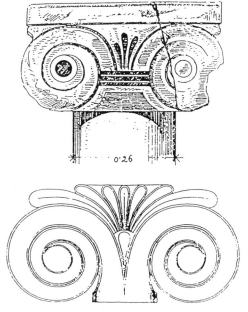

ABOVE & OPPOSITE: Ionic and Aeolean volutes, after J Durm

far as the industry of man could reach, to discover the laws upon which she herself acted in the production of her works in order to transfer them to the business of architecture. Reflecting therefore upon the practice of nature as well with relation to an entire body, as to its several parts, they found from the very first principles of things, that bodies were not always composed of equal parts or members; whence it happens, that of the bodies produced by nature, some are smaller, some larger and some middling: and considering that one building differed from another, upon account of the end for which it was raised, and the purpose which it was to serve, as we have shown in the foregoing books, they found it necessary to make them of various kinds. Thus from an imitation of nature they invented three manners of adorning a building, and gave them names drawn from their first inventors. One was better contrived for strength and duration: this they called *Doric*; another was more taper and beautiful, this they named *Corinthian*; another was a kind of medium composed from the other two, and this they called *Ionic*. Thus much related to the whole body in general. Then observing, that those three things which we have already mentioned, namely the number, finishing and collocation, were what chiefly conduced to make the whole beautiful, they found how they were to make use of this from a thorough examination of the works of nature, and, as I imagine, upon the following principles. The first thing they observed, as to number, was that it was of two sorts, even and uneven, and they made use of both, but in different occasions: for, from the imitation of nature, they never made the ribs of their structure, that is to say, the columns, angles and the like, in uneven numbers; as you shall not find any animal that stands or moves upon an odd number of feet. On the contrary, they made their apertures always in uneven numbers, as nature herself has done in some instances, for although in animals she has placed an ear, an eye, and a nostril on each side, yet the great aperture, the mouth, she has set singly in the middle. [. . .]

BOOK IX
CHAPTER VIII
Some short, but general observations which may be looked upon as laws in the business of building and ornament.
[. . .] The errors of the judgment are both in time and in their nature of much the greatest importance, and when committed, less capable of being remedied. With these therefore we shall begin. The first error is to choose for your structure a region which is unhealthy, not peaceable, barren, unfortunate, melancholy, or afflicted with calamities, either apparent or concealed. The next errors to this are choosing a platform not proper or convenient; adding one member to another, without constant regard to the accommodation of the inhabitants, and not providing fit and suitable conveniences for every rank and degree of them, as well masters as servants, citizens as rustics, inmates as visitants: making your building either too large and spacious or too small and narrow; too open and naked or too much shut in and confined; too much crowded or too rambling with too many apartments, or too few: if there be a want of rooms where you may secure yourself against excessive heats, or excessive colds, of places where you may exercise and divert yourself when you are in health, and of others where you may be sufficiently sheltered against any inclemency of air when you are sick: to which add the structures not being sufficiently strong, and as we may say, fortified to be safe against any sudden attack: if the wall be either so slight as not to be sufficiently strong to support itself and the roof, or much thicker than necessity requires, if the different roofs bespatter each other with their waters, or throw them against any part of the wall, or near the entrances: if they be either too low, or too high: if your windows be too wide, and admit unwholesome winds, noxious dews, or too much burning sun; or on the other hand if they be so narrow as to occasion a melancholy

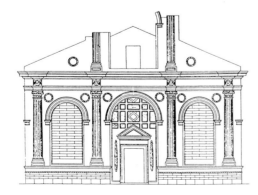

gloom; if they break into any of the ribs of the building: if the passages are any ways obstructed or lead us to any object that is offensive: or in short if any of those other instructions are neglected which we have given in the preceding books. Among the errors in ornament, the principal in architecture as in nature is making anything preposterous, maimed, excessive or any other ways unsightly: for if these things are reckoned defective and monstrous in nature herself, what must we say of an architect that throws the parts of his structures into such improper forms? And as the parts whereof those forms consist, are lines, angles, extension and the like, it is certainly true that there can be no error or deformity more absurd and shocking than the mixing together either angles or lines or superficies which are not in number, size and situation equal to each other, and which are not blended together with the greatest care and accuracy. And indeed who can avoid blaming a man extremely, that without being forced to it by any manner of necessity, draws his wall crooked and askew, winding this way and that like a worm crawling upon the ground, without any rule or method, with one side long and another short, without any equality of angles or the least connection with regard to each other; making his platform with an obtuse angle on one side and an acute one on the other and doing everything with confusion, absurdity and at a venture. [. . .]

Leone Battista Alberti, *Ten Books on Architecture*, translated by James Leoni, edited by Joseph Rykwert (Alec Tiranti, London, 1965).

LEFT: Callicrates, Temple of Athena Nike, Athens, c 427-424 BC, after J Durm; OPPOSITE: LB Alberti, Tempio Malatestiano, Rimini, c 1450, after Quatremère de Quincy, Histoire des plus célèbres architectes, *1830*

IMMANUEL KANT
CRITIQUE OF JUDGEMENT

BOOK I

Analytic of the Beautiful. Third Moment
The judgement of taste, by which an object is described as beautiful under the condition of a definite concept is not pure.

There are two kinds of beauty: free beauty *(pulchritudo vaga)*, or merely dependent beauty *(pulchritudo adhaerens)*. The first presupposes no concept of what the object ought to be; the second does presuppose such a concept and the perfection of the object in accordance therewith. The first is called the beauty of this or that thing; the second, as dependent upon a concept, is ascribed to objects which come under the concept of a particular purpose.

Flowers are free natural beauties. Hardly anyone but a botanist knows what sort of a thing a flower ought to be; and even he, though recognising in the flower the reproductive organ of the plant, pays no regard to this natural purpose if he is passing judgment on the flower by taste. There is, then, at the basis of this judgment no perfection of any kind, no internal purposiveness, to which the collection of the manifold is referred. Many birds (such as the parrot, the humming bird, the bird of paradise) and many sea shells are beauties in themselves, which do not belong to any object determined in respect of its purpose by concepts, but please freely and in themselves. So also foliage for borders or wall papers, mean nothing in themselves; they represent nothing – no object under a definite concept – and are free beauties. We can refer to the same class what are called in music phantasies (ie pieces without any theme), and in fact all music without words.

In the judging of a free beauty (according to the mere form), the judgment of taste is pure. There is presupposed no concept of any purpose which the manifold of the given object is to serve, and which therefore is to be represented in it. By such a concept the freedom of the imagination which disports itself in the contemplation of the figure would be only limited.

But human beauty (ie of a man, a woman, or a child), the beauty of a horse, or a building (be it church, palace, arsenal, or summer house), presupposes a concept of the purpose which determines what the thing is to be, and consequently a concept of its perfection; it is therefore adherent beauty. Now as the combination of the pleasant (in sensation) with beauty, which properly is only concerned with form, is a hindrance to the purity of the judgment of taste, so also is its purity injured by the combination with beauty of the good (viz that manifold which is good for the thing itself in accordance with its purpose).

We could add much to a building which would immediately please the eye if only it were not to be a church. We could adorn a figure with all kinds of spirals and light but regular lines, as the New Zealanders do with their tattooing, if only it were not the figure of a human being. And again this could have much finer features and a more pleasing and gentle cast of countenance provided it were not intended to represent a man, much less a warrior. [. . .]

OPPOSITE: WL Bottomley, Garden steps at Milbourne House, Richmond, Virginia, c 1935

BOOK II
Analytic of the Sublime
The relation of genius to taste

[. . .] A beauty of nature is a *beautiful thing*; beauty of art is a *beautiful representation* of a thing.

In order to judge of a natural beauty as such, I need not have beforehand a concept of what sort of thing the object is to be; ie I need not know its material purposiveness (the purpose), but its mere form pleases by itself in the act of judging it without any knowledge of the purpose. But if the object is given as a product of art and as such is to be declared beautiful, then, because art always supposes a purpose in the cause (and its causality), there must be at bottom in the first instance a concept of what the thing is to be. And as the agreement of the manifold in a thing with its inner destination, its purpose, constitutes the perfection of the thing, it follows that in judging of artificial beauty the perfection of the thing must be taken into account; but in judging of natural beauty (as *such*) there is no question at all about this. [. . .]

Beautiful art shows its superiority in this, that it describes as beautiful things which may be in nature ugly or displeasing. The Furies, diseases, the devastations of war, etc, may be described as very beautiful, as they are represented in a picture. There is only one kind of ugliness which cannot be represented in accordance with nature without destroying all aesthetical satisfaction, and consequently artificial beauty, viz that which excites *disgust*. For in this singular sensation, which rests on mere imagination, the object is represented as it were obtruding itself for our enjoyment, and thus it is impossible that it can be regarded as beautiful. [. . .]

Immanuel Kant, *Critique of Judgement*, translated by JH Bernard (Collier Macmillan Publishers, London and Hafner Press, New York, 1951).

RIGHT: Vestibule to Peribolus of Eleusis, capital of the antae, after JJ Hittorff; OPPOSITE: Asklepieion at Pergamum, detail of theatre

GE LESSING
LAOCOÖN

PREFACE

The first person to compare painting with poetry was a man of fine feeling who observed that both arts produced a similar effect upon him. Both, he felt, represent absent things as being present and appearance as reality. Both create an illusion, and in both cases the illusion is pleasing.

A second observer, in attempting to get at the nature of this pleasure, discovered that both proceed from the same source. Beauty, a concept which we first derive from physical objects, has general rules applicable to a number of things: to actions and thoughts as well as to forms.

A third, who examined the value and distribution of these general rules, observed that some of them are more predominant in painting, others in poetry. Thus, in the one case poetry can help to explain and illustrate painting, and in the other painting can do the same for poetry.

The first was the amateur, the second the philosopher, and the third the critic.

The first two could not easily misuse their feelings or their conclusions. With the critic, however, the case was different. The principal value of his observations depends on their correct application to the individual case. And since for every one really discerning critic there have always been fifty clever ones, it would have been a miracle if this application had always been made with the caution necessary to maintain a proper balance between the two arts.

If Apelles and Protogenes, in their lost writings on painting, confirmed and explained its laws by applying already established rules of poetry, we may be certain that they did so with the same moderation and accuracy with which the principles and lessons of painting are applied to eloquence and poetry in the works of Aristotle, Cicero, Horace, and Quintilian. It is the prerogative of the ancients never to have done too much or too little in anything.

But in many respects we moderns have considered ourselves far superior when we transformed their pleasant little lanes into highways, even though shorter and safer highways themselves become mere footpaths as they lead through wildernesses.

The brilliant antithesis of the Greek Voltaire [Simonides of Ceos, died 496 BC] that painting is mute poetry and poetry a speaking painting was doubtless not to be found in any textbook. It was a sudden fancy – among others that Simonides had – and the truth it contains is so evident that one feels compelled to overlook the indefinite and untrue statements which accompany it.

The ancients, however, did not overlook them. In restricting Simonides' statement to the effect achieved by the two arts, they nevertheless did not forget to stress that, despite the complete similarity of effect, the two arts differed both in the objects imitated as well as in the manner of imitation.

Still, many recent critics have drawn the most ill-digested conclusions imaginable from this correspondence between painting and poetry, just as though no such difference existed. In some instances they force poetry into the narrower limits of painting; in others they allow painting to fill the whole wide sphere of poetry. Whatever one is entitled to must be permitted to the other also; whatever pleases or displeases in one must necessarily please or displease in the other. And so, full of this idea, they pronounce the shallowest judgments with the greatest self-assurance and, in criticising the work of a poet and a painter on the same subject, they regard the differences of treatment observed in them as errors, which they blame on one or the other, depending on whether they happen to prefer painting or poetry.

Indeed, this spurious criticism has to some degree misled even the masters of the arts. In poetry it has engendered a mania for description and in painting a mania for allegory, by attempting to make the former a speaking picture, without actually knowing what it could and ought to paint, and the latter a silent poem, without having considered to what degree it is able to express general ideas without denying its true function and degenerating into a purely arbitrary means of expression.

To counteract this false taste and these unfounded judgments is the principal aim of the following chapters. They were written as chance dictated and more in keeping with my reading than through any systematic development of general principles. Hence they are to be regarded more as unordered notes for a book than as a book itself. [. . .]

I should like to remark, finally, that by 'painting' I mean the visual arts in general; further, I do not promise that, under the name of poetry, I shall not devote some consideration also to those other arts in which the method of presentation is progressive in time.

CHAPTER V

[. . .] The idea of having the father and his two sons connected in one entanglement by means of the deadly serpents is undeniably an inspired one and gives evidence of a highly artistic imagination. Whose was it, the poet's or the artist's? [. . .]

The poet has described the serpents as being of marvellous length. They have wound their huge coils around the boys and seize the father, too, when he comes to their aid. [. . .] Because of their size, they could not have unwound themselves from the sons at once; there must therefore have been a moment when they had already attacked the father with their heads and front parts while still holding the sons encircled with their hind parts. This moment is necessary to the progress of the poetic picture; the poet allows us to feel it completely, but this was not yet the time to depict it in full detail. [. . .]

The poet is careful to leave Laocoön's arms free from the coils which have encircled his body, and thus his hands have perfect freedom. [. . .] In this point the artists necessarily had to follow his example. Nothing is more expressive and lively than the action of the hands; especially when emotions are in play, the most mobile face is meaningless without such movement. Arms locked to the body by the serpents' coils would have cast an air of stillness and death over the whole group, but we see the arms in full freedom, both in the principal and the secondary figures; and their activity is greatest where the pain is most violent.

But this freedom of the arms was the only point in regard to the coiling of the serpents that the artists found expedient to borrow from the poet. Virgil winds the serpents twice around the body and neck of Laocoön and has their heads project high above him. [. . .]

This picture satisfies our imagination fully; the most essential parts of the body are squeezed to the point of strangulation, and the venom is aimed toward the face. However, this is no picture for the artist, whose object is to show the physical effects of the venom and the pain. To show these effects the vital parts must be left as free as possible and external pressure completely avoided, for this might change and weaken the activity of suffering nerves and labouring muscles. The double

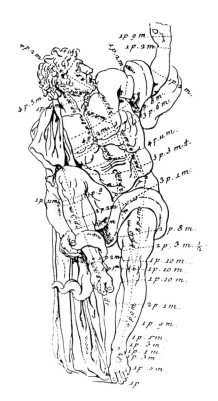

ABOVE & OPPOSITE: Details of statue of Laocoön, after Diderot and D'Alembert, L'Encyclopédie, *c 1750s*

coils would have concealed all of the trunk, and the painful contraction of the stomach, which is so expressive, would have been invisible. Those parts still exposed above or below or between the coils would have been seen amid constrictions and distensions caused not by inner pain but by the external pressure. So many coils around the neck would have destroyed the pyramidal effect of the group, which is so pleasing to the eye, and the pointed heads of the serpents projecting from the mass into the air would have been such a violation of proportion as to render the effect of the whole extremely repulsive. Some designers have nevertheless been foolish enough to follow the poet too closely. And, as we might expect, the disgusting results can be seen only too clearly in an engraving by Franz Cleyn, to take one example. The ancient sculptors saw immediately that their art required a completely different treatment. They transferred all the coils from the body and neck to thighs and feet, where they could conceal and squeeze as much as necessary without detriment to the expression, and where at the same time they could awaken the idea of suddenly arrested flight and a kind of immobility which is highly advantageous to the apparent continuation of that posture.

I do not know why the critics have treated with complete silence this difference between the serpents' coils in the statue and in the poem. It reveals the wisdom of the artists just as much as another difference which they have all recognised but have attempted to justify rather than ventured to praise. I refer to the difference in regard to clothing. Virgil's Laocoön is clad in his priestly robe while in the statue he and his sons appear naked. Some people, I am told, find it absurd for a king's son and a priest to be represented in this way at a sacrificial ceremony. To these objectors art critics answer in all earnestness that it is a departure from conventionality, to be sure, but the artists were forced to this because they could not attire the figure appropriately. Sculpture, they say, cannot imitate fabrics; thick folds produce a bad effect; and so one must choose the lesser evil and violate truth rather than be censured because of the drapery. If ancient artists had smiled at the objection, I cannot imagine what their reaction to the reply would have been. Nothing could be more disparaging to the arts than this remark. For even if we supposed that sculpture could imitate fabrics as well as painting, would it have been necessary for Laocoön to be clad? Would we lose nothing by this drapery? Is a garment, the work of our poor human hands, as beautiful as an organic body, the work of eternal wisdom? Does it require the same talents, is it of the same merit, does it bring just as much honour to imitate the former as it does the latter? Is it only deception that our eyes require, and is it a matter of indifference to them with what they are deceived?

In poetry a garment is not a garment; it conceals nothing; our imagination sees right through it. Whether Virgil's Laocoön wears robes or not, his suffering is just as evident in one part of the body as in another. To the imagination his brow is encircled but not hidden by the priestly fillet. Indeed, this fillet is not only no hindrance, it actually strengthens the idea we form of the sufferer's misfortune. [. . .] His priestly dignity avails him nothing. Even its emblem, which assures him honour and respect everywhere, is soaked and desecrated by the poisonous slaver.

But the artist must give up this subordinate association of ideas if the main theme is not to suffer. Had he left Laocoön so much as the fillet he would have greatly weakened the expression, for the brow, the seat of expression, would have been partly covered. As in the case of the scream he sacrificed expression for beauty, here he gives up conventionality for expression. On the whole, conventionality was considered quite unimportant by the ancients. They felt that the highest aim of their art called for a complete rejection of conventionality. Beauty was their highest goal; necessity was the inventor of clothing, and what has art to do with necessity? I grant that there is also such a thing as beauty in clothing, but what is

that when compared to the beauty of the human form? And will he who can attain the greater be content with the lesser? I fear that the greatest master in the rendering of drapery shows by this very talent wherein his weakness lies. [. . .]

CHAPTER VII

When we say that the artist imitates the poet or the poet the artist, we can mean one of two things: either that the one takes the other's work as his model, or that both work from the same model and one borrows his manner of presentation from the other.

When Virgil describes the shield of Aeneas, he is 'imitating' the artist who made it, in the first meaning of the term. The work of art, not what is represented in it, is his model, and even if at the same time he describes what we see represented in it, he is only describing it as a part of the shield and not as the thing itself. But if Virgil had imitated the statue of Laocoön, this would have been an imitation in the second meaning of the term. For he would have imitated not the statue, but what the statue represents, and only the details of his imitation would have been borrowed from the statue.

In the first case the work of the poet is original, in the second it is a copy. The first is a part of that general imitation which is the very essence of his art, and whether his subject is a work of other arts or a work of nature, he creates as a genius. But the second kind robs him completely of any dignity. Instead of representing the thing itself, he imitates an imitation and gives us lifeless reflections of the style of another man's genius rather than his own. [. . .]

CHAPTER XI

[. . .] As a matter of fact, the poet who treats of a well-known story or well-known characters has a great advantage. He can omit the hundred pedantic details which would otherwise be indispensable to an understanding of the whole; and the sooner he makes himself understood to his audience, the more quickly he can arouse their interest. The artist has this advantage, too, when his subject is not new to us, when we recognise at first glance the intent and meaning of his entire composition, and when we not only see that his characters are speaking, but also hear what they are saying. The greatest effect depends on the first glance, but if this forces us into laborious reflection and guessing, our desire to be moved is immediately cooled. In order to avenge ourselves on the incomprehensible artist we harden our feelings against the expression of the figures, and woe to him if he has sacrificed beauty for expression! In such a case we find nothing that induces us to linger before his work. What we see we do not like; and what the artist wants us to think, we do not know.

Let us consider both these points together: firstly, invention and originality are by no means the most important things that we demand of the painter; secondly, a well-known subject promotes and renders more accessible the effect of his art. The reason why artists so seldom select new subjects should not be sought, as Count Caylus does, in indolence, or ignorance, or in technical difficulties of his art. We shall find the reason more deeply founded and perhaps be inclined to praise in the artist as wise self-restraint useful to ourselves what at first appears to be a limitation of art and an interference with our pleasure.

Gotthold Ephraim Lessing, *Laocoön: An Essay on the Limits of Painting and Poetry*, translated by Edward Allen McCormick (The John Hopkins University Press, Baltimore and London, 1984).

ABOVE & OPPOSITE: Draped figures and Expressions of passions, after Diderot and D'Alembert

133

GWF HEGEL
AESTHETICS

PART III
CHAPTER II
2 The Particular Determinants of the Architectural Forms
(a) *Building in Wood and Stone*

It has already been mentioned earlier that there has been a long dispute about whether what was original was building in wood or in stone, and whether architectural forms derived from this difference. In architecture proper it is purpose that dominates, and the fundamental type of the house is developed into beauty, and for this reason wooden construction may be assumed to be the earlier.

This Hirt assumed and he has often been criticised. My own view on this disputed question I will state briefly. [. . .] Hirt looks for a basic model for Greek buildings, as it were for the theory of them, their anatomical structure, and he finds it, its form and corresponding material, in the house and in building in wood. Now of course a house as such is built principally as a dwelling, as a protection against wind, rain, weather, animals, and men, and it requires a complete enclosure where a family or a larger community can assemble, shut in by themselves, and pursue their needs and concerns in this seclusion. A house is an entirely purposeful structure, produced by men for human purposes. So the builder has many aims and concerns in the course of his work. In detail the frame, in order to be supported and stable, has to connect various joints and thrusts together in line with mechanical principles, and observe the conditions imposed by weight and the need for stabilising the structure, closing it, supporting its upper parts, and, in general, not merely carrying these but keeping the horizontal horizontal and binding the structure together at recesses and corners. Now a house does demand a total enclosure for which walls are the most serviceable and safest means, and from this point of view building in stone seems to be more appropriate, but a sort of wall can equally well be constructed from stanchions set alongside one another on which beams rest and these at the same time bind together and secure the perpendicular stanchions by which they are supported and carried. Finally, on top of these is the ceiling and the roof. Apart from all this the chief point in the temple, God's house, on which everything turns is not the enclosure but the carrying beams and what they carry. For this mechanical matter building in wood proves to be the first and the most appropriate to nature. [. . .]

Without any need for extensive and difficult workmanship, the tree affords both stanchions and beams, because wood has already in itself a definite formation; it consists of separate linear pieces, more or less rectangular, which can be directly put together at right, acute, or obtuse angles, and so provide corner-columns, supports, cross-beams, and a roof. On the other hand, stone does not have from the start such a firmly specific shape, but, compared with a tree, is a formless mass which, for some purpose must be split and worked on before the separate stones can be brought together and piled on one another, and before they can be built

OPPOSITE: Temple of Amenhotep III, Luxor, c 1370 BC

together into a unity again. Operations of many kinds are required before it can have the shape and utility that wood has in and by itself from the start. Apart from this, stone in huge blocks invites excavation rather, and, in general, being relatively formless at the start, it can be shaped in any and every way and therefore it affords manageable material not only for symbolic but also for romantic architecture and its more fantastic forms; whereas wood owing to its natural form with rectilinear stems is directly more serviceable for the severer purposiveness and mathematical proportions that are the basis of classical architecture. [. . .]

But, conversely, classical architecture does not stop at all at building in wood but proceeds on the contrary, where it develops into beauty, to build in stone, with the result that while in its architectural forms the original principle of building in wood is still always recognisable, specific characteristics nevertheless enter which are not inherent in building in wood as such.

(b) *The Specific Forms of the Temple*

As for the chief particular points concerning the house as the fundamental model for the temple, the most essential things to be mentioned here are limited in brief to what follows. [. . .]

The first thing of importance in this connection affects load-bearing. As soon as load-bearing masses are mentioned, we generally think first, in view of our present-day needs, of a wall as the firmest and safest support. But, as we said already, a wall as such does not have supporting as its sole principle, for on the contrary it serves to enclose and connect and for this reason is a preponderating feature in romantic architecture. The peculiarity of Greek architecture is at once seen to consist in the fact that it gives shape to this supporting as such and therefore employs the column as the fundamental element in the purposiveness of architecture and its beauty.

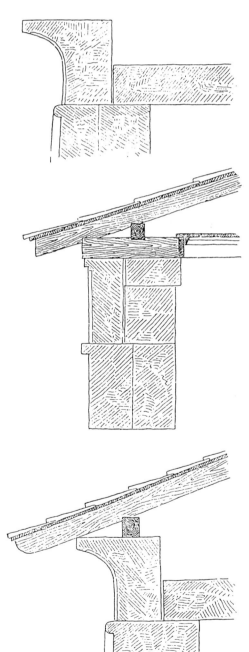

The column has no other purpose but to be a support and, although a row of columns set up beside one another in a straight line marks a boundary, it does not enclose something as a solid wall or partition does but is moved in front of a proper wall and placed by itself independently. Where the aim is exclusively that of serving as a support, it is above all important that in relation to the load resting on it the column should have the look of being there for a purpose and therefore should be neither too weak nor too strong, should neither appear compressed nor rise so high and easily into the air as merely to look as if it were playing with its load.

Just as the column is distinguished on one side from an enclosing wall and a partition, so on the other side it is distinguished from a mere stanchion. The stanchion is planted directly on the ground and ends just as directly where the load is placed on it. Therefore its specific length, its beginning and end seem as it were to be a negative limitation imposed by something else, or to be determined accidentally in a way not belonging to it on its own account. But beginning and ending are determinations implicit in the very nature of a column as a support and on this account must come into appearance on it as constituent features of its own. [. . .]

If the beginning of the column is not to seem vague and accidental, it must be given on purpose a foot on which it stands and which expressly reveals the beginning to us as a beginning. By this means art intends, for one thing, to say to us: 'Here the column begins,' and, for another thing, to bring to the notice of our eye the solidity and safety of the structure and, as it were, set our eye at rest in this respect. For the like reason art makes the column end with a capital which indicates the column's real purpose of load-bearing and also means: 'Here the column ends.' This reflection on the intentionally made beginning and end provides the really deeper reason for having a pedestal and a capital. It is as if, in music, there were a cadence without a firm conclusion, or if a book did not end with a full stop or begin without the emphasis of a capital letter. In the case of a book, however, especially in the Middle Ages, large decorative letters were introduced (at the beginning) and decorations at the end to give objectivity to the idea that there was a beginning and an end. [. . .]

As for further details about the shape of the column beyond the pedestal and capital, the *first* point is that it is round, like a circle, because it is to stand freely, closed in on itself. But the circle is the simplest, firmly enclosed, intelligibly determinate, and most regular line. Therefore by its very shape the column proves that it is not intended, set up with others in a thick row, to form a flat surface in the way that stanchions, cut square and set alongside one another, make up walls and partitions, but that its sole purpose is, within its own self-limitation, to serve as a support. *Secondly,* in its ascent the shaft of the column tapers slightly, usually from a third of its height; it decreases in circumference and diameter because the lower parts have to carry the upper, and this mechanical relation between parts of the column must be made evident and perceptible. *Finally,* columns are usually fluted perpendicularly, partly to give variety to the simple shape in itself, partly, where this is necessary, to make them look wider owing to this division of the shaft.

Now although a column is set up singly on its own account, it nevertheless has to show that it is not there for its own sake but for the weight it is to carry. Since a house needs to be bounded on every side, a single column is insufficient; others are placed alongside it and hence arises the essential requirement that columns be multiplied or form a row. Now if several columns support the same weight, this carrying a weight in common determines their common and equal height, and it is this weight, the beam, which binds them together. This leads us on from load-carrying as such to the opposite constituent, the load carried.

What the columns carry is the entablature laid above them. The first feature arising in this connection is the right angle. The support must form a right angle alike with the ground and the entablature. For by the law of gravity, the horizontal position is the only one secure and adequate in itself, and the right angle is the only fixedly determinate one, while the acute and obtuse angles are indeterminate, variable, and contingent in their measurement.

The constituent parts of the entablature are organised in the following way:

On the columns of equal height set up beside one another in a straight line there immediately rests the architrave, the chief beam which binds the columns together and imposes on them a common burden. As a simple beam it requires for its shape only four level surfaces, put together at right-angles in all dimensions, and their abstract regularity. But although the architrave is carried by the columns, the rest of the entablature rests on it, so that it in turn is given the task of load-carrying. For this reason, architecture in its advance presented this double requirement on the main beam by indicating through projecting cornices, etc, the load-carrying function of its upper part. So regarded, the main beam, in other words, is related not only to the loadbearing columns but just as much to the other loads resting on it.

These loads are first of all the frieze. The band or frieze consists of (a) the ends of the roof-beams lying on the main beams and (b) the spaces between these. In this way the frieze contains more essential differences in itself than the architrave has and for this reason has to emphasise them in a more salient way, especially when architecture, though carrying out its work in stone, still follows more strictly the type of building in wood. This provides the difference between triglyph and metope. Triglyphs, that is to say, are the beam-ends which were cut thrice on the frieze, while metopes were the quadrangular spaces between the individual triglyphs. In the earliest times these spaces were probably left empty but later on they were filled, indeed overclad and adorned with bas-reliefs.

The frieze which rests on the main beam carries in turn the crest or cornice. This has the purpose of supporting the roofing which ends the structure at the top. At

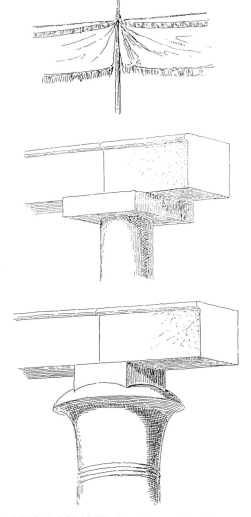

ABOVE & OPPOSITE: Egyptian and Greek eaves details. Tent and post-and-lintel construction. After C Uhde

once the question arises about the sort of thing that this final boundary must be. For in this matter a double kind of boundary may occur, a right-angled horizontal one or one inclined at an acute or obtuse angle. If we look at requirements, it appears that southerners who have to suffer very little from rain or stormy winds need protection from the sun only, so that they can be satisfied with a horizontal and right-angled roof for a house. Whereas northerners have to protect themselves from rain which must be allowed to run off, and from snow which should not be allowed to become too heavy a load; consequently they need sloping roofs. Yet architecture as a fine art cannot settle the matter by requirements alone; as an art it has also to satisfy the deeper demands of beauty and attractiveness. What rises upwards from the ground must be presented to us with a base, a foot, on which it stands and which serves as a support; besides, the columns and walls of architecture proper give us materially the vision of load-carrying. Whereas the top, the roof, must no longer support a load but only be supported, and this character of *not* supporting must be visible on itself, ie it must be so constructed that it *cannot* now support anything and must therefore terminate at an angle, whether acute or obtuse. Thus the classical temples have no horizontal roof, but roof surfaces meeting at an obtuse angle, and the termination of the building in this way is in conformity with beauty. For horizontal roofs do not give the impression of a completed whole, for a horizontal surface at the top can always carry something else, whereas this is not possible for the line in which sloping roof-sides meet. What satisfies us in this respect is the pyramidal form which is satisfying in painting too, eg, in the grouping of its figures.

The final point for our consideration is enclosure, ie walls and partitions. Columns are indeed load-carrying and they do form a boundary, but they do not enclose anything; on the contrary, they are the precise opposite of an interior closed on all sides by walls. Therefore if such a complete enclosure is required, thick and solid walls must be constructed too. This is actually done in the building of temples.

About these walls there is nothing further to mention except that they must be set up straight and perpendicular to the ground, because walls rising at acute or obtuse angles give the eye the impression of impending collapse, and they have no once and for all settled direction because it may appear to be a matter of chance that they rise at this or that acute or obtuse angle and no other. Adaptation to a purpose and mathematical regularity alike demand a right-angle here once again.

Walls can both enclose and support, while we restricted to columns the proper function of supporting only. Consequently this at once suggests the idea that, when the different needs of enclosure and support are both to be satisfied, columns could be set up and unified into walls by thick partitions, and this is the origin of half- (or embedded-) columns. [. . .]

But the real column is essentially round, finished in itself, and expresses precisely by this perfection that it is a contradiction to continue it with a view to making a level surface and therefore a wall, out of it. Consequently, if supports are wanted in walls, they must be level, not round columns but flat things which can be prolonged to form a wall. [. . .]

The column must have its foot in front of the wall and come forward independently of it. In modern architecture we do often have the use of pilasters, but these have been regarded as a repeated shadow of earlier columns and have been made not round but flat. Hence it is clear that although walls can also carry, still, since the task of carrying is already borne by columns, they have, on their part, in developed classical architecture, to make enclosure their essential aim. [. . .]

ABOVE: *Corinthian capital from the choragic monument of Lysicrates, after J Durm; OPPOSITE: Birth House (Mammisi) near the Temple of Hathor, Dendera, Greco-Roman period*

Georg Wilhelm Friedrich Hegel, *Aesthetics: Lectures on Fine Art*, Vol II, translated by TM Knox (Clarendon Press, Oxford, 1975).

QUATREMERE DE QUINCY
ON IMITATION IN THE FINE ARTS

PART I
CHAPTER I
Definition of the Elementary Principle of Imitation in the Fine Arts

The imitative faculty is truly characteristic of man; it is concerned in all his acts, it enters into all his works; among all creatures it belongs to him, and to him alone, in such wise that he may be defined by this property, in naming him the *imitative animal*. Hence, the numberless different significations in which the word *imitation* is employed; hence, the variety of imitative effects which are continually produced in all the works of human industry; and hence, consequently, the necessity of isolating the theory of *imitation in the fine arts*, and submitting it to an especial investigation. [. . .]

I reduce this fundamental principle to its most simple expression in the following terms: *To imitate in the fine arts, is to produce the resemblance of a thing, but in some other thing which becomes the image of it.*

By this definition may be at once distinguished the essential difference that exists between the imitation which is proper to the fine arts, and the other kinds of imitation.

To produce certain resemblances belongs, without doubt, to every kind of imitation. But even though all imitation produces resemblances, all resemblance is not therefore necessarily a result of imitation; which is self-evident, as, for instance, in the works of nature in which are found the greatest number of resemblances, and those the most striking. It is sufficient to name any one of those numerous objects which she is perpetually reproducing. The word reproduce expresses that power which she possesses of bringing forth a countless number of organised bodies, which, succeeding each other in the same forms and with the same properties, must in consequence frequently present a very great similarity. Every one is aware that in all this there is no imitation. It is not nature that imitates; it is she that is imitated.

Nearly the same thing holds good, of the resemblances which exist among what are called the works of human industry. Man also brings forth objects, which, by reproducing, he multiplies in order to supply the wants of society. But these objects resemble each other without, on that account, begetting in us either impressions or pleasure such as arise from the resemblances, which the imitation of the fine arts produces.

It may truly be affirmed that the idea of the similarity which exists between one ear of corn and another, between one fruit and another on the same tree, in no wise affects us. In like manner no agreeable emotion arises within us at the innumerable resemblances which may be found among the manufactured productions of human industry. Everyone will say that such would assuredly be the case, because, in the first instance, that of natural productions, the resemblance is the result of organic power, and, in the second, of a mechanical operation.

Undoubtedly: but that is not sufficient.

Why does not this sort of organic or mechanical repetition equally give rise in us to the idea of resemblance or imitation, and, above all, to the pleasurable emotion which is attached to that idea?

The reason is, simply because that which constitutes the primary condition of imitation is wanting; namely, the *image*. [. . .]

The arts are then distinguished from one another by the difference of their efficient model, by the difference of their instruments, and by that of the faculties or organs that nature has placed in reciprocal relation with them.

It follows from the evidence that determines their distinctiveness, that it is impossible for any one of them, in its own respective attributes, to add to its imitative resemblance the means and effects which belong to the imitative resemblance of another. [. . .]

I will here adduce an instance, and will select it from the two arts most nearly approaching one another. I mean painting and sculpture, both having for their object the imitation of bodies, and both being addressed to the same organ, that of sight. Now what have these in common? The one represents bodies by their colour, and the other by the relief of their forms. Nevertheless, the model which serves for both, unites relief and colour, and these two are blended so intimately together, that they can be divided only in thought.

Without any exception, that art which employs colour, cannot aspire to relief; nor can that which appropriates to itself relief aim at truth of colouring. What then is it that prevents these two from uniting? Many moral reasons may be given; but I will instance one wholly material or technical.

It is this: that provided colour could be applied to the figure of the statuary, the colouring would no longer be that of the painter. For if the attempt were made, even with the utmost skill, to lay on the sculptured head the tints of the coloured one, the elements of both would be opposed to each other. The colouring of a picture is only such in painting: let it be removed from the canvas, and it loses everything, in losing the fictitious atmosphere, which is the condition of its effect. Artificial colour upon an isolated body can never appear true, precisely because all around it being real can serve only to convict it of falsity.

Thus, imitation is nullified by the very endeavours that are made to increase or multiply its means; and thus one art, by trenching on the properties of another, loses its own, and by aiming to be both, becomes neither.

CHAPTER VI
[. . .] The erroneous idea too frequently entertained concerning imitation in the fine arts, the kind, and still more the degree, of resemblance, which it belongs to each of those arts to produce, leads the majority of persons to believe, that the more numerous are the sorts of resemblance comprised by a single art, the more lively will be the pleasure derived from its works. Hence the tendency on all hands to seek to advance the arts beyond the bounds of their own particular domain, and, encroaching on the legitimate province of the neighbouring art, to appropriate more or less some part of the imitative resemblance which by nature is denied them. [. . .]

CHAPTER IX
First Error of the Artist
It consists in stepping beyond his own art to seek, in the resources of another, an increase of imitative resemblance.

CHAPTER X
Second Error of the Artist

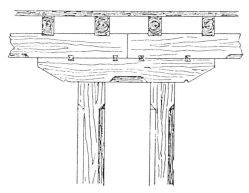

ABOVE & OPPOSITE: The origins of the distylon in timber bracket construction, after C Uhde

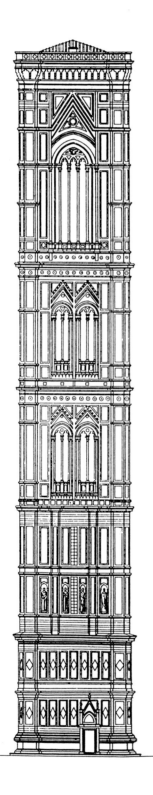

It consists in seeking truth short of the limits of every art, by a system of servile copy, which deprives the imitation or the image, of that fictious part which constitutes at once its essence and its character.

[In this case, the artist] has no other aim, within his restricted horizon, than that of identifying his work with the individual model. He labours to bring it to such a point as to give it the semblance of being traced. He exchanges the charm attached to the fictiousness of appearance, for the disenchantment of a false truth; in short, the freedom of an imitation for the servileness of a copy. [. . .]

It will be sufficient to advert to those deviations of taste which have prevailed at certain periods, and in certain schools, when the artist conceived that he was faithfully imitating nature, by reproducing, as in a mirror, the deformities which belonged only to the individual he had for his model, by reducing the works of imitation to a mere impress, a kind of *fac simile* destitute of beauty, and deprived of every characteristic of true imitation. [. . .]

CHAPTER XI

In every art [therefore] there must be, with respect to truth, some fiction, and, with respect to resemblance, something incomplete.

If it be true that each of the fine arts can only comprehend a part of the great and universal model, and can only reproduce that portion corresponding with the means that are appropriate to it, by what is termed an image, one is compelled to acknowledge that the imitation granted by nature to every imitative mode, must necessarily remain incomplete as regards similarity, and fictious in what appertains to truth. [. . .]

CHAPTER XII

It is the fictious and the incomplete in every art, and these alone, which constitute art, and become moreover the sources of the pleasure of imitation.

Since, by the laws of nature, an art can be nothing else than a manner of seizing and presenting a single aspect of the universal model, nothing can be more futile than any effort on the part of the artist to give to his image an additional truth, or an increase of resemblance elicited from a source beyond the sphere of its imitation. [. . .]

Of a truth, it is the *fictious* and *incomplete* in every art that constitute it art. It is thence that it derives its principal force, and the effect of its action. And thence, too, proceeds its power of giving pleasure. [. . .]

CHAPTER XV

The pleasure of imitation is proportionate to the distance which, in every art or imitative mode, and in the works of each, separates the elements of the model from those of the image.

[. . .] We have already seen that the mind finds no pleasure in that surreptitious imitation which, being no other than a repetition of the thing to be imitated, re-becomes, as it were, the thing itself; and it appears to us that the true reason of that want of pleasure is the state of inactivity in which the mind continues, unmoved by every, so deemed, work of imitation which gives no exercise to the faculty of comparison. [. . .]

PART III
CHAPTER II
Of Convention Understood as a Mean of Imitation

By comparing the action of each art, in its relations with ourselves, to a game having its rules, and being in fact no longer played when either party ceases to conform to them, we showed that in like manner there are between imitation and man, certain reciprocal conditions, constituting the devices of this species of game and the means of playing it. Its end is not gain, but pleasure; and this pleasure, like gain, may be either lawful or unlawful. The same circumstances that render the gain unlawful, disannuls the game also. That which disannuls the pleasure of imitation tends also to render void, on either part, the conditions under faith of which the effect must be attained and received.

Custom has assigned the name of *conventions* to the various sorts of compact that hold good between imitation and man, and which the very nature of things has occasioned. Conventions are, theoretically speaking, the means of imitation, since without them, it could have no ground for operation. Moreover, they are very numerous.

Almost everything with respect to art is founded on conventions, if it be true that all art is itself really a convention.

It will be recollected, for instance, that we have already represented the fine arts as placed around their common model, in such a position as to allow of each one comprehending no more than a single side – a single aspect. It is precisely this limited position that occasions the physical or moral impossibility of reproducing in the image the totality of the model, and consequently renders necessary the means of convention established between ourselves and art; their effect is to prevent us from perceiving the imperfection arising from what is wanting to imitation in order to its being complete, and also to prevent its impression from being too much weakened. [. . .]

Antoine Chrysostome Quatremère de Quincy, *An Essay on the Nature, the End, and the Means of Imitation in the Fine Arts*, translated by JC Kent, (1979 facsimile, reprint of the 1837 edition, by Smith, Elder and Co, London).

LEFT: The development of the plinth base and of trabeated and arcuated construction, after C Uhde; OPPOSITE: Giotto (later A Pisano and F Talenti), The Campanile, Florence, 1334-59, after Quatremère de Quincy

EUGENE-EMMANUEL VIOLLET-LE-DUC
LECTURES ON ARCHITECTURE

LECTURE ONE

[. . .] A man of greater intelligence and strength than his neighbours has killed a lion. He hangs its skin above the doorway of the cave which he inhabits. This commemorative spoil perishes; he therefore cuts in the stone, as best he can, something which resembles a lion, that his children and neighbours may preserve the remembrance of his strength and courage. But he wishes this sign, destined to perpetuate the memory of his valour, to be seen from afar – to attract notice. He has observed that red is the most striking of all colours; he therefore daubs his sculptured lion with red. To all who see this image it plainly says: 'Here is the dwelling of the strong man who knows how to defend himself and his.' This is Art. Here it exists entire, complete, needing only to perfect its means of execution.

Our primitive hero dies. His family hew out a cell in the rock wherein to deposit his remains, and above it they carve a man fighting with a lion. The figure of the man will be large, that of the lion small; for the relatives of the deceased wish passers-by to know that the father or the husband represented was a man of might. True, a little man who kills a great lion is more courageous than a man of great stature who overpowers a wild beast of small size; but this is a complex idea which does not enter into the mind of the primitive artist. In all the ancient sculptured monuments of India, and even of Egypt, the conqueror is represented as of colossal size and the enemies he has vanquished as pigmies. [. . .]

LECTURE SIX

[. . .] In the present day we are no longer familiar with those simple and true ideas which lead artists to invest their conceptions with style; I think it necessary therefore to define the constituent elements of style, and in so doing, carefully to avoid equivocal terms, and those meaningless phrases which are repeated with the profound respect that is professed by most people for what is incomprehensible. Ideas must be presented in a palpable form – a definite embodiment – if we would communicate them. Clearly to understand what style as regards form is, we must consider form in its simplest expressions. Let us therefore take one of the primitive arts – one of the earliest practised among all nations, because it is among the first needed – the art of the coppersmith, for example. It matters little how long it took man to discover the method of refining copper, and of reducing it to thin plates, so as to make a vessel with it fit to contain liquid. We take the art at the time when he had discovered that by beating a sheet of copper in a particular way he could so model it as to give it the form of a vessel. To effect this, all the workman needs is a piece of iron as a point of support, and a hammer. He can thus, by beating the sheet of copper, cause it to return on itself, and of a plane surface make a hollow body. He leaves a flat circular bottom to his vessel, so that it may stand firm when full. To hinder the liquid from spilling when the vessel is shaken, he contracts its upper orifice, and then widens it out suddenly at the edge, to facilitate pouring out

the liquid; the most natural form therefore [is] that determined by the mode of fabrication. There must be a means of holding the vessel: the workman therefore attaches handles with rivets. But as the vessel must be inverted when empty, and has to be drained dry, he makes the handles so that they shall not stand above the level of the top of the vessel. Thus fashioned by methods suggested in the fabrication, this vessel has style: first, because it exactly indicates its purpose; second because it is fashioned in accordance with the material employed and the means of fabrication suited to this material; third, because the form obtained is suitable to the material of which this utensil is made, and the use for which it is intended. This vessel has style, because human reason indicates exactly the form suitable to it. The coppersmiths themselves, in their desire to do better or otherwise than their predecessors, deviate from the line of the true and the good. We find therefore a second coppersmith, who wishes to alter the form of the primitive vessel in order to attract purchasers by the distinction of novelty; he gives a few extra blows of the hammer, and rounds the body of the vessel which had hitherto been regarded as perfect. The form is in fact new, and all the town wish to have vessels made by the second coppersmith. A third coppersmith, perceiving that his fellow-townsmen are taken with the rounding of the base, goes still further, and makes a third vessel, which is still more popular. This last workman, having lost sight of the principle, bids adieu to reason, and follows caprice alone; he increases the length of his handles, and advertises them as of the newest taste. This vessel cannot be placed upside down to be drained without endangering the shape of these handles; but everyone praises it, and the third coppersmith is credited with having wonderfully improved his art, while in reality he has only deprived a form of its proper style, and produced an unsightly and relatively inconvenient article.

This history is typical of that of style in all the arts. Arts which cease to express the want they are intended to satisfy, the nature of the material employed, and the method of fashioning it, cease to have style. [. . .]

LECTURE NINE

[. . .] It is not necessary to have seen many Greek buildings, Ionian and Dorian, to perceive that in the architecture of these populations the designing of mouldings was regarded as one of the essential parts of art; and that the designs were not the results of caprice, but of just reasoning and a refined sense of form. All the mouldings of the beautiful Greek architecture had been caressed, shall I say, with studious love. Now, in the designs for mouldings, two conditions must be observed: the function they have to perform, and the effect to be produced in the place they occupy. A moulding is good only in as far as it exactly fulfils these conditions. The material employed may modify the design without thereby changing the principle. It is natural to give greater delicacy and even thinness to a moulding cut in marble than to one worked in a friable stone; but this is a question of more or less sharpness given to the angles – of more or less depth given to the sinkings. The principles are the same for both. But it would denote a condition of profound barbarism to give, for example, to mouldings of joiner's work the section adapted for those that suit stone or marble – to mouldings inside a hall the section adapted to those outside it. The artists of the Middle Ages did not, any more than the Greeks, forget these very natural laws; I would say again that the former pushed still further than their predecessors the rigorous observance of principles, at any rate as far as we can judge from the few Greek buildings that remain. With the Greeks, as in our architecture of the twelfth century, the moulding serves three purposes: it either supports a projection, or it forms a footing, or it marks a height, or defines an opening. In the first case the moulding is a cornice; in the second a base, a basement, a plinth; in the third a string-course, a jamb, a frame. Except for these three functions, a moulding has no rational purpose; accordingly, it does not

ABOVE: Timber framed house among the Aryas of the Upper Indus, after Viollet-le-Duc, Histoire de l'habitation humaine, *1876; OPPOSITE: Primitive, modified and bad forms of copper vessels, after Viollet-le-Duc,* Entretiens sur l'architecture, *1872*

appear otherwise in good Greek architecture, any more than in French medieval architecture. These functions being thus determined, mouldings are reduced to three elementary arrangements – shapings, shall I say, dictated by the necessity of the structure. But this shaping admitted, It remains to give these projections the forms suitable to their purpose, and the place they occupy. They have a use, and should produce a certain effect in accordance with that use. The cornice, if external, should protect the outer walls, and throw off the rain-water far from their surface; as all the under part is in shade, it should be worked in such a manner as to appear sufficiently strong to sustain the projection. The string-course is only a cincture, indicating either the level of a floor or a change in the building of the faces; it is a projecting course which should appear able to resist a pressure and clearly mark a separation. The enframing moulding, the jamb moulding, stays the faces and strengthens the partitions of a void. The base, plinth, or socle sustains all the weight, forms a footing on the ground, and serves as a transition between the horizontal and the vertical plane.

Examine some of these mouldings designed by the Greek architects. Figure [I] presents mouldings of capitals, antae, and cornices. A is the cornice moulding of the temple of Castor and Pollux at Agrigentum; this is an exterior moulding; beneath the gutter *b* is hollowed out the throat *c*, intended to hinder the rain-water from spreading along the drip; then comes the drip *d*, which arrests the light and also throws off the water. The numbers *e* are sharply accentuated in order to give dark lines beneath the shadow thrown by the drip. These mouldings therefore serve a purpose, and are intelligible to the eye. The great gutter moulding will catch the luminous rays at *g*, and will also present two dark lines above that line of light to give it projection. Similarly, buried in the shadow cast by this gutter moulding, a second dark line *c* will bring out the transparency of that shadow. If we direct a luminous ray on this moulding, at an angle of 45°, for instance, we should remark that the artist obtains two fine luminous lines, at *h* and *g*, separated by dark lines; and a third dark line at *c*, to limit, as it were, the shadow thrown by the gutter; and beneath the great shadow of the drip other strongly marked lines which variegate that broad belt of shadow with ledges and grooves admirably calculated to intensify it here and diminish it there, as they court or shun reflected lights.

Here, then, we have study of effect together with provision for a requirement. The moulding of the antae of the temple of Neptune at Paestum, drawn at B, completely buried in the shadow of the pronaos, is, on the contrary, designed to receive a reflected light, as indicated by the wide ogee moulding *b'*; there again we remark the sunk-in dark line *c'* beneath the reflected light taken by the upper member. The same may be said of the moulding C, crowning the architrave of the interior order. The moulding D of the propylaea of Eleusis is likewise designed in reference to a reflected light. It will be observed that the upper fillet *j* falls slightly back in order to show out the reflected light of the chamfer *j'*, that the face *i* inclines a little to take the light, that the torus *k* recedes near the horizontal part of the abacus for shadow and to set off the projection of the latter, that this torus is abruptly cut to produce a sharp shadow at *l*, that, lastly, between the vertical face *m* and that shadow *l*, there is a transition accentuating a reflex increasing in brightness as it approaches the torus, and that this reflex is cut by shades and bright lines so as to fill up the curved surface and give it value. The section E of a portion of frieze from the temple of Ceres at Eleusis gives us another example of the delicacy with which the Greeks designed their mouldings intended to receive only reflected light. [. . .]

Here [Figure II] are some Greek base mouldings. These mouldings are evidently designed to be seen from above. They spread out on the ground, lead the eye from the vertical line to the horizontal plane, and are only accentuated by the fine scotias *a*, or by sinkings that give sharp shadows to define the toruses. It will be observed

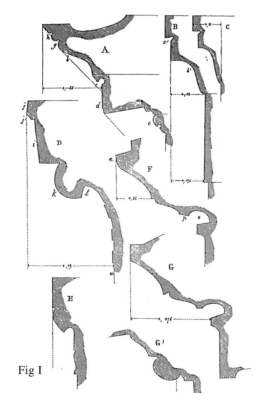

Fig I

how, in the moulding E, the upper torus is flattened in its lower part to disengage the fillet *b*. The shape of the lower torus *c* of the moulding G, which we give to a larger scale at *c'*, should also be remarked. [. . .]

LECTURE FIFTEEN

[. . .] One of the conditions of beauty in an architectural work is that it should impress all who see it as having been produced naturally without effort, without occasioning trouble or anxious consideration to its designer, that in fact it could not have been otherwise. In particular, it should be free from those expedients that betray paucity of ideas – those *bits* which bear the mark of studied effort, and the aim on the part of the designer to astound and engage the attention of the passers-by without being able to satisfy his mind. To be clear, to be comprehensible without requiring an effort: this is, and always will be, the aim which the architect should have in view. [. . .] Similarly, in viewing the work of the architect, everyone should experience the impression that the materials in combination do but reflect the anticipation of the beholder – that the conception as realised is the only one that was appropriate to the circumstances of the case. [. . .]

Eugène-Emmanuel Viollet-le-Duc, *Lectures on Architecture*, Vols I and II, translated by Benjamin Bucknall, (Dover Publications, New York, 1987).

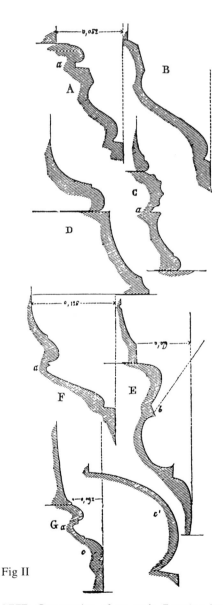

Fig II

LEFT: Construction of an early Egyptian house, after Viollet-le Duc, Histoire de l'habitation humaine, *1876; ABOVE & OPPOSITE: Profiles of classical Greek cornices and bases, after Viollet-le-Duc,* Entretiens sur l'architecture, *1872*

GOTTFRIED SEMPER
THE FOUR ELEMENTS OF ARCHITECTURE

THE FOUR ELEMENTS (1851)

[. . .] The first sign of human settlement and rest after the hunt, the battle, and wandering in the desert is today, as when the first men lost paradise, the setting up of the fireplace and the lighting of the reviving, warming, and food-preparing flame. Around the hearth the first groups assembled; around it the first alliances formed; around it the first rude religious concepts were put into the customs of a cult. Throughout all phases of society the hearth formed that sacred focus around which the whole took order and shape.

It is the first and most important, the *moral* element of architecture. Around it were grouped the three other elements: the *roof*, the *enclosure*, and the *mound*, the protecting negations or defenders of the hearth's flame against the three hostile elements of nature.

According to how different human societies developed under the varied influences of climate, natural surroundings, social relations, and different racial dispositions, the combinations in which the four elements of architecture were arranged also had to change, with some elements becoming more developed while others receded into the background. At the same time the different technical skills of man became organised according to these elements: *ceramics* and afterwards metal works around the *hearth, water* and *masonry works* around the *mound, carpentry* around the *roof* and its accessories.

But what primitive technique evolved from the *enclosure*? None other than the art of the *wall fitter (Wandbereiter)*, that is, the weaver of mats and carpets. This statement may appear strange and requires an explanation.

It was mentioned previously that there are writers who devote much time to searching for the origin of art and who believe they can deduce from it all the different ways of building. The nomadic tent plays a rather important role in their arguments. Yet while with great acumen they detect in the catenary curve of the tent the norm of the Tartar-Chinese way of building (although the same shapes occur in the caps and shoes of these people), they overlook the more general and less dubious influence that the carpet in its capacity as a *wall*, as a vertical means of protection, had on the evolution of certain architectural forms. Thus I seem to stand without the support of a single authority when I assert that the carpet wall plays a most important role in the general history of art.

It is well known that even now tribes in an early stage of their development apply their budding artistic instinct to the braiding and weaving of mats and covers (even when they still go around completely naked). The wildest tribes are familiar with the hedge-fence – the crudest wickerwork and the most primitive pen or spatial enclosure made from tree branches. Only the potter's art can with some justification *perhaps* claim to be as ancient as the craft of carpet weaving.

The weaving of branches led easily to weaving bast into mats and covers and then to weaving with plant fibre and so forth. The oldest ornaments either derived

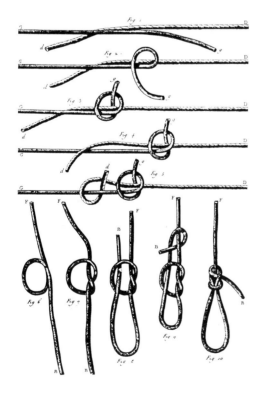

from entwining or knotting materials or were easily produced on the potter's wheel with the finger on the soft clay. The use of wickerwork for setting apart one's property, the use of mats and carpets for floor coverings and protection against heat and cold and for subdividing the spaces within a dwelling in most cases preceded by far the masonry wall, and particularly in areas favoured by climate. The masonry wall was an intrusion into the domain of the wall fitter by the mason's art, which had evolved from building terraces according to very different conditions of style.

Wickerwork, the original space divider, retained the full importance of its earlier meaning, actually or ideally, when later the light mat walls were transformed into clay tile, brick, or stone walls. Wickerwork was the *essence of the wall*.

Hanging carpets remained the true walls, the visible boundaries of space. The often solid walls behind them were necessary for reasons that had nothing to do with the creation of space; they were needed for security, for supporting a load, for their permanence, and so on. Wherever the need for these secondary functions did not arise, the carpets remained the original means of separating space. Even where building solid walls became necessary, the latter were only the inner, invisible structure hidden behind the true and legitimate representatives of the wall, the colourful woven carpets.

The wall retained this meaning when materials other than the original were used, either for reason of greater durability, better preservation of the inner wall, economy, the display of greater magnificence, or for any other reason. The inventive mind of man produced many such substitutes, and all branches of the technical arts were successively enlisted.

The most widely used and perhaps the oldest substitute was offered by the mason's art, the stucco covering or bitumen plaster in other countries. The woodworkers made panels with which to fit the walls, especially the lower parts. Workers handling fire supplied glazed terracotta and metal plates. As the last substitute perhaps can be counted the panels of sandstone, granite, alabaster, and marble that we find in widespread use in Assyria, Persia, Egypt, and even in Greece. [. . .]

STYLE IN THE TECHNICAL AND TECTONIC ARTS (1860)
The Knot

The knot is perhaps the oldest technical symbol and, as I have shown, the expression for the earliest cosmogonic ideas that arose among nations.

The knot serves, first of all, as a means of tying together two ends of cord, and its strength is chiefly based on the resistance of friction. The system that best promotes friction by lateral pressure when the two cords are pulled in opposite directions along their length is the strongest. Another condition occurs when pressure is exerted on the cords not in the direction of length but perpendicular to their extension, although even in this case the resultant of the tension is best considered as moving in the longitudinal direction of the cords. The weaver's knot is the strongest and most useful of all knots, perhaps also the oldest or at least the first that figured in the technical arts. The rope maker and sailor know a great number of knot systems, on which, unfortunately, I can only speak as a layman. Related to the description of these systems are other things that would be of interest to our interpretation, but these also must be left to more expert hands.

A very ingenious and ancient application of the knot led to the invention of the network, which even the most savage tribes know how to make and use for fishing and hunting. The mesh of the net, whose knot is illustrated here, has the advantage that a damaged mesh does not affect the whole system and is easily mended. This is, at the same time, the criterion for the network, which in other respects permits the most diverse variations but in this particular point remains the same under all

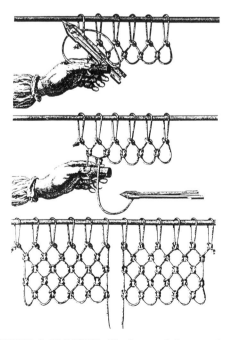

ABOVE & OPPOSITE: The knot and the net, after Diderot and D'Alembert

conditions. Spanish hemp was considered the best for nets in antiquity. Cumean hemp was also famed in this regard. The ancients made nets in which wild boars were caught, but of such great fineness that a single man could carry enough of them on his back to surround an entire forest. Yet the same netting in a thicker mesh also served as a corselet, in which each thread, although fine in itself, was sewn together from three hundred to four hundred individual fibres. This industry appears to have prospered especially in Egypt. The Egyptians also made decorative nets from glass-bead necklaces, of which several charming examples have survived. This ornament was also prevalent among Greek women, as well as among Etruscan and Roman women. In India the net serves as a rich motif for head coverings and necklaces that are admirable in the alteration of the mesh and in the distribution of the decorations and pendants. The Middle Ages loved the network, and the Spanish have retained the time-honoured value of delicate networks as adornments for the hair and as a very light wrap.

In architecture, in ceramics, and generally in all the arts, the net is used for the decoration of surfaces, and is often applied in a structural-symbolic way as an adornment on projecting and bulging parts, for example, on the paunch of vases. [. . .]

Plaiting (The Plait, Braid, Seam, Canework, Mat)
Plaiting should perhaps have been mentioned before knitting among the textile arts. Next to twisted yarn, it is the product used in making yarn, yet it also serves for making integuments. Plaiting provides a stronger system of cords than twisted yarn, since the individual cords that compose it act more in their natural direction, that is, in the direction of absolute strength when they are in tension. It also has the advantage that it is not so easily 'unravelled', that is, to loosen its elementary threads. For a plaiting at least three cords are needed, alternately interwoven. Yet the cords can be increased by any number, although in making a plaiting never more than three primary and repeating cords are active at any one time, following definite laws by which the cords that had been active are dropped and successively picked up by others. The round plaiting produces the torus and is very useful in saddlery. It also serves as a braid in the haberdasher's art and is generally used, as already noted, as a very handy cord for the strongest yarns, for instance, in making anchor cables. With rigid materials, like metal wire, it is the best way to bind many wires into one. This system of cord is capable of the richest ornamental development and almost absolute elegance. Therefore, it was with good reason that the mother of the human race probably chose it as a hair adornment, and it is likely that through this agency the plait became one of the earliest and most useful symbols of the technical arts that architecture borrowed. The plait lends itself equally well to cylindrical and circular surfaces, while the idea of binding is always present by an association of ideas. This is decisive for the use and proper application of the plait. The modality and intensity of the band also becomes expressed to some extent by the type and strength of the applied ornamental plaiting. The maximum strength, for instance, is expressed by that rich strap network found on the bases of Attic-Ionic columns and in other places.

I must leave further details concerning the aesthetics of these interesting products of the textile art to educated haberdashers, saddlers, and above all to hair stylists, the last of whom, in fact, have attained everything possible in the technical perfection of the plait and have thereby controlled the taste of whole centuries.

Plaiting, by virtue of its absolute strength, is not only suited to be effective when stretched lengthwise; it can also serve as a *seam* to connect two sections of a dress and as such becomes active across the direction of extension. As a seam, plaiting forms a wonderfully rich motif for ornamental play in all the handicrafts and even in architecture, as was already shown above. [. . .]

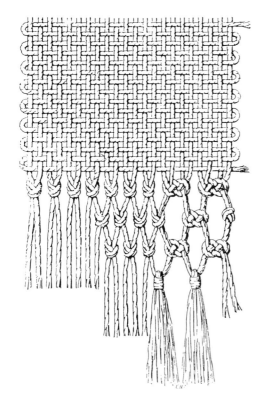

Plaiting already appears in the last-named products as *surface-creating*; it fulfills this purpose still more emphatically in the actual *mat* (the plaited cover).

One advantage plaited covers have over woven ones is that the cord elements out of which they are fashioned do not necessarily have to intersect at right angles, as is imposed by weaving, but cords running diagonally and in any direction can be interwoven into the texture. *This advantage of plaiting should be maintained in every way, made apparent, and be stressed as a characteristic feature.*

The art of making covers from cane is very old and has made no essential technical advances since the Old Kingdom of the Pharaohs. Nevertheless, in their aesthetic understanding of the motif, the Egyptians of that time were, as are now the North American Iroquois and many other savage and half-savage tribes, more spontaneous, more fortunate, and more ingenious than we modern Europeans with our admired mechanical omnipotence.

The wicker mat produces the richest variety of geometrical patterns, especially when the elements are varied by colour changes and in size. It was always a prolific motif for surface decoration in Egypt and Assyria, the last of whose glazed brick walls were often patterned on models of wicker mats, especially around the time of the later dynasties of the Assyrian Empire (Khorsabad and Kuyunjik). Following the time-honoured tradition, the same motif was used to excess in the Asiatic-Byzantine style and in the various branches of the Arabian style. It received its highest development in Spain under the Moorish caliphs. All lower wall surfaces were panelled with such a patterned, glazed tile.

The Renaissance, especially in the handicrafts (pottery, tarsia, metalworks) but also in painted decorations, returned to this Arabian motif, which incidentally had been introduced into Europe once before in the Romantic period of the eleventh and twelfth centuries (Norman churches in Sicily and Normandy, in several motifs of the Saxon-Romantic style, the Doge's Palace in Venice). Presently, we shall discuss the predilection of the Chinese and the Indians for wickerwork and its importance for the primordial history *(Urgeschichte)* of architecture and style.

ON ARCHITECTURAL STYLES (1869)

[. . .] However, permit me to set forth in a short definition what I wish to be understood by the term *style*.

Style is the accord of an art object with its genesis, and with all the preconditions and circumstances of its becoming *(Werden)*. When we consider the object from a stylistic point of view, we see it not as something absolute, but as a result. Style is the *stylus*, the instrument with which the ancients used to write and draw; therefore, it is a very suggestive word for that relation of form to the history of its origin. To the tool belongs, in the first place, the hand that leads it and a will that guides the hand. These, then, intimate the technical and personal factors in the genesis of a work of art. Thus, the hammering of metal, for example, requires another style than the casting of metal. One can also say Donatello and Michelangelo are related in style, and so forth. Both are equally correct.

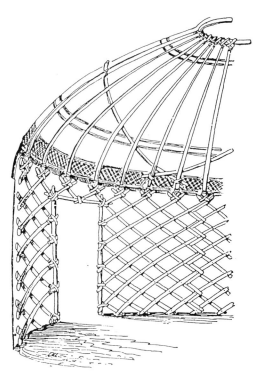

In addition to the tool and the hand that guides it, there is the material to be treated, the formless mass to be transposed into form. In the first place, every work of art should reflect in its appearance, as it were, the material as physical matter. Thus, for example, the Greek temple in marble differs in style from an otherwise, almost identical Greek temple in porous stone. In this way we may speak of a wood style, a brick style, an ashlar style, and so forth. [. . .]

Gottfried Semper, *The Four Elements of Architecture and Other Writings*, translated by HF Mallgrave and W Herrmann, (Cambridge University Press, Cambridge and New York, 1989).

ABOVE & OPPOSITE: Plaited wickerwork and weaving used for enclosing walls and partitions, after G Semper, Der Stil, 1860-63

HEINRICH TESSENOW

HOUSE BUILDING AND SUCH THINGS

Technical Form

[. . .] If we think of a rich, but particularly empty ornament and place next to it a copper cable carrying a high voltage, then we have two opposed forms of human work: in the first case a lot of form without there being really anything behind it, in the second case almost no form, yet an enormous amount being contained. In the end we deny both equally, what we are looking for is a form which is alive in all its parts, but also allows all living things to express themselves fully. We negate the ornament as much as we negate the copper cable with the high voltage which is not expressed. Both forms are, as such, inferior, but nowadays we generally have a greater respect for the copper cable. It interests us more, we have a greater affinity towards it. It bears greater hope, for it has more to do with the rational than the ornament, and our world today, so topsy-turvy and full of colour, compels us strongly to respect the rational. Surely it is not irrelevant that we should ask 'why' so often, even when we know that it is stupid to keep on asking. But in the search for primary, simple or necessary things we become hostile to form. Hence, we have largely the same aspirations for technology as we have for the machine. It is certainly not the technical or machine-like form itself we love, though there are numerous truly naked technical forms which immediately appeal to our hearts: the form of a yacht, or a bicycle, for instance. We certainly value the simple technical form overwhelmingly for the economic values it nurtures in us. We can value the technical form very highly, yet still not want to have water pipes mounted visibly on the walls of our rooms, and we feel similarly on thousands of issues. The form of the electricity generator is not a matter of total indifference to us, but that is not saying much. After all, we are never completely indifferent to anything.

On the one hand, in technical or machine-like work today we place exceptional value on the search for concise form. On the other hand, we value the quality of repetition in the machine-like form because our largest and most important task is to orient ourselves. If we always see familiar things, or if we see very little, then our orientation may remain crude; but here we are dealing with something basic – industrial work suffers from nothing so much as the fear of the fundamental crudeness on which its refinements are always based. To take an example, the precise church tower is based on raw boulders, and the fine medieval masonry is based on a simple knowledge of the crafts, and the fine mature medieval work of the craftsman is itself based on a hard social order. The high esteem in which we hold a simple school-like form of knowledge as a fundamental quality will help bring out the best in our industrial work. This is also the result of the high esteem in which we hold simple technical and mechanical work. [. . .]

Order

[. . .] Order is most effectively shaped through repetition, and just as industrial work requires order to prosper, so it also requires uniformity.

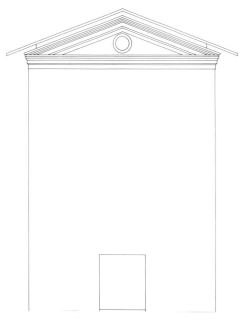

ABOVE: Sigurd Lewerentz, Resurrection Chapel, Enskede Cemetery, Stockholm, c 1921-23; OPPOSITE: Mnesicles, The Propylaea, Athens, 437-432 BC, after J Durm

A deliberately uniform work brings our more refined formative forces into operation. In the case of something completely new these forces fail; therein lies the blessing which the recognition of order has for all simple abilities.

In order to cope with the world, or in order to recognise it when dealing with it, it is necessary to concentrate our senses on the finer details. For example, a shepherd who seeks to differentiate between the sheep in his large grey flock, will find it necessary to note minute differences which vary the appearance of the individual sheep, and he is able to do so. Because we are not shepherds all sheep look the same to us – our eyes are blunted to any refinements.

However, uniformity partially shapes the senses; we have to experience a lot of similar things if we are to recognise fine differences between them and therein lies a limitation corresponding to that which is contained in order.

The more we recognise the uniformity of our work and the less we require our work to be entirely new, the more refined will it become in its formation. In the same way the similarity of men's clothing allows us to be aware of their refinements – this is true of men's clothing to a far greater extent than it is of women's, where refinements in terms of the cut, the tailoring, the choice of colour and so forth are extremely rare. The rapidly changing differences of the overall work means a rare ability is required for refinements beyond the necessary whole to be attained. [. . .]

Hence a strong normative quality in our houses and our pieces of furniture is not just a good thing in itself, it is a question of repeating what is an essentially correct quality. Indeed, to achieve such a thing today is probably very difficult. What is important here is that we lose the fear we often have of order and repetition and the uniform *per se*. [. . .] There is no doubt that they belong to today's healthy and strong means of production. We fear the idiosyncratic but not the familiar or the normative. [. . .]

Heinrich Tessenow, *Hausbau und dergleichen*, translated by Wilfried Wang, *(9H*, London, 1989).

I N D E X